A Short History
of Migration

— A Short History — of Migration

—Massimo Livi-Bacci—

Translated by Carl Ipsen

polity

First published in Italian as *In cammino* © Società editrice Il Mulino, Bologna, 2010

This English edition © Polity Press, 2012

The translation of this book has been funded by SEPS – SEGRETARIATO EUROPEO PER LE PUBBLICAZIONI SCIENTIFICHE

Via Val d'Aposa 7 - 40123 Bologna - Italy
seps@seps.it - www.seps.it

Polity Press
65 Bridge Street
Cambridge CB2 1UR, UK

Polity Press
350 Main Street
Malden, MA 02148, USA

ISBN-13: 978-0-7456-6186-5
ISBN-13: 978-0-7456-6187-2(pb)

A catalogue record for this book is available from the British Library.

Typeset in 11 on 13 pt Sabon
by Toppan Best-set Premedia Limited

The publisher has used its best endeavours to ensure that the URLs for external websites referred to in this book are correct and active at the time of going to press. However, the publisher has no responsibility for the websites and can make no guarantee that a site will remain live or that the content is or will remain appropriate.

Every effort has been made to trace all copyright holders, but if any have been inadvertently overlooked the publisher will be pleased to include any necessary credits in any subsequent reprint or edition.

For further information on Polity, visit our website: www.politybooks.com

Contents

Preface

In 1960, I crossed the Atlantic aboard the ocean liner *Queen Frederica*, of the National Hellenic American Line, and so witnessed first hand the last phase of the great European migration. The aging ship followed the Piraeus–Naples–New York route and carried some of the last Greek and Italian immigrants making their way to the US after entry restrictions had been temporarily loosened following World War II. I traveled with them, along with other Fulbright students, in third class. The year I spent in the States helped me to understand a society that owed its birth and expansion to immigration. I spent a month on Long Island with an American family of Sicilian origin and a year at Brown University in Providence, Rhode Island, the only state at the time that did not have a Protestant majority, owing to Italian, Portuguese, Greek, and French-Canadian immigration. In the US, migration was a normal and accepted phenomenon: a source of tension, of course, but a founding force of American society. In Italy, it was a time of heavy migration: internal, to Europe, and that final flow overseas. And there the emigration debate focused instead on how to alleviate the poverty that lay at its root, to soften its harsh consequences. Emigration was seen as a pathology: a failure and the price paid for backwardness. The dominant political and cultural debate did not contemplate the possibility that those Italian emigrants would, as a group, rapidly escape out from under the weight of poverty. These two views of migration seem contradictory, but they are simply reflections of the two sides of the phenomenon: departure and arrival.

This book seeks to posit and prove a conviction that shapes both its substance and the nature of the study undertaken: territorial movement is a human prerogative and an integral part of human capital; it is one of many ways that the human species has sought to improve its living conditions. It is an innate quality that has assured the survival of hunter-gatherers, the expansion of the species across the continents, the spread of agriculture, the settlement of open spaces, world integration, and the first globalization of the nineteenth century. We can also describe this prerogative as a form of adaptability or fitness. This fitness – an intertwining of biological, psychological, and cultural characteristics – has not been constant over historical epochs or even during specific migrations. For example, the settlement of open spaces required individuals inclined to form solid families tied to traditional values, individuals who would have many children and work hard, providing the fuel for further expansion. The migration of the last two centuries has instead been different: often directed to urban areas and engaged in trade and industrial work, it has favored single and culturally flexible individuals who instead created relatively small families. The birth of political nations or states and the drawing up of national borders converted migrations into international movements and so spawned migration policies, namely, the intervention by governments (or powerful lords or other institutions) to direct, plan, and encourage migrations. These policies reduced to a greater or lesser extent the free choice of migrants. They were based on the presumption that under current circumstances higher powers could judge the fitness of migrants better than the migrants themselves. In some cases, attempts were made to increase that fitness, supplying resources, knowledge, or other advantages. Results varied and might be successful or catastrophic. We consider examples of both in the pages that follow.

In the modern era, even before the Industrial Revolution, movement became easier – resources increased, technology improved, infrastructures were consolidated – as internal and international migration systems developed. Navigation of the oceans tied together Eurasia, Africa, and the Americas. Starting in 1500, Europe became a net exporter of human capital, following millennia during which it had been a target for immigration and invasion. Meanwhile, the ability and inclination of states to interfere in individual choices regarding migration increased. Migration accelerated, reaching truly massive proportions in the nineteenth century. The slow pace of agricultural migration gave way to faster and more intense migration flows that had profound effects on both the sending and receiving countries. The past century, instead, from World War I to the present day, has been characterized by irregular progress, contradictory policies, the shock of two world wars, the temporary separation of Eastern and Western Europe, the inversion of the migration cycle – Europe has once again become an importer of human capital – and the profound impact of the so-called demographic transition (declining mortality and fertility). In recent decades, immigration policies have grown progressively more restrictive and more selective as immigration pressure has increased, a function of both demographic and economic differences between North and South. The prerogative of migrants has been weakened. Migration is seen as a price to be paid for demographic decline, as a remedy for labor-market bottlenecks, as an emergency in need of resolution, as a looming threat. Migrants are more and more viewed simply as labor rather than as an integral part of the societies they join. Never before has the conflict of interests between sending countries, receiving countries, and the migrants themselves been more evident. Much has been done to increase and regulate economic trade; nothing has been done to govern migration. When it comes to migration, states hold tenaciously to the concept of national sovereignty, refusing to cede even a bit of authority to super-national bodies. And yet some sort of global governance and cooperation is sorely needed if those competing interests are to be reconciled, and if we want to restore to migration that positive role it has always played in human development.

I have studied migration intermittently over the course of my career, starting with the research I undertook after that trip on the *Queen Frederica*, and following up with various studies over the subsequent decades. These pages constitute an attempt to bring together reflections, insights, and notes I have collected during that career. They are based, again, on the understanding that migration is a human prerogative and so a normal constitutive element of any society.

– 1 –
Waves of Progress and Gradual Migration

Man has spread widely over the face of the earth, and must
have been exposed, during his incessant migration, to the
most diversified conditions. The inhabitants of Tierra del
Fuego, the Cape of Good Hope, and Tasmania in the one
hemisphere, and of the arctic regions in the other, must
have passed through many climates, and changed their
habits many times, before they reached their present
homes.[1]

Moreover, that same humanity described here by Charles
Darwin originated in equatorial Africa; and its methods of
survival, ways of life, and habits had to continually evolve
in order to make settlement possible in those more extreme
corners of the two hemispheres. Darwin's passage, two
centuries after his birth, reminds us of the role migration
has played – from the origins of humanity up to the present
day – in the geographic distribution of the human race,
the growth of population, and the ever-changing circumstances of life. Migration has been a key element of social
and biological evolution. Nonetheless, in the twenty-first
century, the great migrations are frequently viewed not as
a primary driving force of social change, but instead as an

anarchic social force, a mismatched tile that cannot find its place in the larger mosaic, interference that disturbs the regular course of everyday life.

Two complementary forces contributed to the gradual occupation of the earth by humans: the ability to reproduce and grow demographically, and the ability to move, that is, to migrate. We do not fully understand how these forces operated: whether smoothly over time or in periodic jumps; when they sped up and when they slowed down. We do know that they contributed to the ability of humans to adapt to changing environmental circumstances, both in nature and climate. Moreover, they were accompanied by complex selection mechanisms so that the characteristics of those who moved on were not identical to those of the others who stayed behind. Rather than become embroiled in a field outside our own expertise, however – and one in which scientific controversy continues to rage – we shall limit ourselves to the fairly straightforward conclusion that migration is an innately human characteristic, and that it has promoted the diffusion, consolidation, and growth of the human species.

Modern human beings spread across the globe from Africa into Western Asia and Europe and then into Eastern Asia, finally reaching the Americas and Australia in the final stages of expansion.[2] That expansion was achieved by moving into areas previously uninhabited, or else occupied by humans with less developed abilities (such as the Neanderthals in Europe). The first Siberian hunters to venture towards the East and traverse the land bridge which emerged between Asia and America during the last Ice Age, some 20,000 or more years ago, were the forerunners of a long and slow march from Alaska to Tierra del Fuego. According to some scholars, occupation of the entire American continent, from the far-flung Northern regions to the most distant Southern lands, occurred in a relatively short span of time, perhaps in just a few thousand years.[3]

We can speak with more assurance about the Neolithic Revolution and the emergence of agriculture in the Near East and Europe. It was a process that began 9,000 years ago in the Fertile Crescent and continued until about 5,000 years ago, when farming reached the British Isles. There are two theories that seek to explain this process, though neither is mutually exclusive and a synthesis of the two is certainly possible. The first theory attributes the spread of agriculture to a process of cultural diffusion. In this case, ideas, practices, and techniques spread across territory. The other theory, that of "demic diffusion," holds that it was not the ideas and practices that spread but the farmers and cultivators themselves, migrants sustained by robust demographic growth. The combination of demographic growth and migration would have set in motion a slow but continuous "wave of progress."[4]

Archaeological dating of European sites where populations developed a sedentary, grain-based system of agriculture is consistent with this theory. The populating of the European continent appears to have occurred along a South–East to North–West axis – from the Eastern Mediterranean to the British Isles – which brought with it the cultivation of new lands and the settlement of new villages. It was a slow wave of progress fueled by demographic growth and the availability of unsettled lands; it advanced at a rate of roughly 1 kilometer per year.[5] This expansion resembled that of the Bantu people who, in migrating from their point of origin along the border of Cameroon and Nigeria, gradually occupied central and southern Africa over the course of three millennia and cultivated a swath of land running from north to south for a distance of 5,000 kilometers.[6]

These prehistoric migrations – both the more rapid movement of hunter-gatherers and the slower spread of agriculture – occurred in unoccupied or very sparsely populated areas. The migrants rarely if ever came in contact with other human inhabitants and were not forced to compete for resources. Over the past 2,000 years, instances of this sort of unopposed expansion have become rarer and rarer. As areas became more densely settled, migrants had to interact and coexist with local populations, possibly imposing their own lifestyle or else adopting the one they encountered as a function of force and circumstance. The process of migration can generate conflicts, confrontations, intermingling, and amalgamation – of a cultural, social, and bio-demographic nature. Naturally, all this occurs over a very drawn-out period of time. At the beginning of the Common Era (0 CE), geographic Europe – the land that lies between the Atlantic and the Urals, the North Sea and the Mediterranean – counted perhaps 30 or 40 million inhabitants, with roughly one-twentieth of its current density and many empty or sparsely populated regions, regions that by the eve of the Industrial Revolution were far less extensive. Many of the migratory movements that characterized Europe in the first millennium of the modern era were movements of invasion and settlement, like the spread of the Germanic peoples following the fall of the Roman Empire. These were intrusions by groups that were small relative to native populations and driven by ambitions of conquest. Overall, they would have comprised only a few percentage points of the native populations.[7] Over this past millennium, European migratory currents have continued to be active: for example, the intense migration towards the East that not even the demographic depression caused by the pandemic of the fourteenth century could stop completely, and that indeed continued until the nineteenth century. It was a process of gradual settlement by the Germanic peoples in lands that had been occupied by Slavs over the previous millennium. In addition to this major migration, there were also many other minor movements: that from north to south following the *Reconquista* of the Iberian Peninsula, or the northward movements of the Scandinavian people, or the southward path taken by Russian migrants in search of a more stable frontier.[8] In the *Reconquista*, the new territories were large while the population of the conquering Christian kingdoms was small, and their settlement in those regions was not a function of land hunger but instead responded to military and political considerations. New settlements were not always stable and were often established at the expense of older communities. It was a case of too much land for too few people, who moreover were often poorly equipped and organized. At the other end of the continent, instead, the Scandinavian people not only expanded inward toward the heart of the European continent, but also toward areas that were less hospitable and climatically challenging. In the ninth century, the Norwegians, united under Harald Fairhair, occupied Iceland: an extraordinary document, the *Landnámabók,* dated at around 930, describes a settlement of 30–50,000 people. They also settled in the Shetland and Orkney Islands and later established an unstable colony in Greenland. In addition to these courageous episodes, the establishment of agriculture is documented in the Baltic Islands, in Scania, and in the central lowlands of Sweden.

The great Germanic eastward migration that began in the ninth century and ended due to the crisis of the fourteenth century is a telling case. We pause to consider the events and movements of this period because they provide a model rendered impossible in our crowded modern world. Put simply, the process developed in three directions: southward, following the natural course of the Danube toward the plains of Hungary; laterally, into the open lands of the Low Countries, Thuringia, Saxony, and Silesia, north of the central Bohemian uplands; and northward, skirting the marshlands and German forests that rendered settlement and migration difficult, and so following the Baltic coast and leading to the gradual foundation of cities such as Rostock and Konigsberg. The Slavic settlements then were pushed to the east and heavily encroached upon from the Germanic lands of Austria in the south, Silesia in the center, and Pomerania and Prussia in the north. Beyond these relatively compact areas (which still maintained, to varying degrees, an ethnically Slavic presence), migratory penetration did not come to a halt, but instead became fragmented, branching into the Baltic provinces, Volhynia, the Ukraine, Transylvania, Hungary, and points further east.

Though this process of settlement was, as we shall see, similar to the spontaneous wave of migration that had populated the European continent a few thousand years before, it had one key difference. It was, in fact, a deliberate and intentional process led and organized by a true migration policy. The colonization process was led by princes, like the Margrave of Meissen, bishops, and, later, the Knights of the Teutonic Order, all of whom invested significant resources. The eleventh and twelfth centuries saw the establishment of colonies beyond the border marked by the Elbe and Saale Rivers, eastern frontier of the Carolingian Empire and so the boundary of Germanic settlement. The twelfth century saw the colonization of Holstein, Mecklenburg, and Brandenburg, and, in the thirteenth, migration spread to Eastern Brandenburg, Pomerania, Silesia, and northern Moravia, beyond the Oder line. The settling of Prussia beyond the Vistula reached its apex in the fourteenth century. Though the Germanic expansion did not penetrate Bohemia, inner Pomerania, or Lusatia, the process of eastward expansion continued, despite the setbacks caused by the long demographic crisis of the fourteenth and fifteenth centuries. The pace of colonization can be measured by the growth of new cities and peaked around 1300.

The great eastward migration, the *Drang nach Osten*, was the major wave of medieval migration, but not the only one. Under the influence of constant movement, the European continent took on a fairly stable structure, one that survived the rapid depopulation caused by plague cycles which left many abandoned villages in their wake. A stable and reliable network of houses, villages, castles, and cities came to occupy much of the European continent.

The medieval migration described here raises a number of questions relevant to our discussion. The first concerns the dimensions of this migratory phenomenon, though most of the evidence is conjectural. Study of the available documentary evidence – censuses, registers, town charters, etc. – suggests that the great twelfth-century migration from the German territories into the land between the Elbe and the Oder Rivers consisted of around 200,000 people.[9] The following century saw a migration of similar dimensions, leading to the colonization of lands reaching as far as Pomerania and Silesia. Documentary evidence indicates that between the years 1200 and 1360, around 1,200 villages were founded in Silesia and another 1,400 in Eastern Prussia, for a grand total of 60,000 farms and potentially around 300,000 people.[10] These numbers are relatively small, though they need to be compared to a German population of origin of modest dimensions, just a few million people (around 6 million in the thirteenth century). Even supposing that these estimates are low and that the population flow might have been two or three times greater, we still arrive at very modest rates of migration, no more than one per thousand per annum. Nonetheless, this relatively modest flow had an important "foundation" effect – a few progenitors with many descendants – if we consider that the number of Germanic people living east of the Elbe–Saale line at the end of the nineteenth century was almost 30 million.

At this point we should address some important questions. First: were these eastward movements caused, as is often postulated, by land hunger resulting from the increased density of cultivated areas in the zones of departure, and so from rapid demographic growth? There are various reasons to question this traditional interpretation: population density was indeed low in the zone of departure, especially at the beginning of the migration; the wave of emigration was relatively small as compared to the vigorous natural growth of the period; and there remained sparsely occupied areas close to home. Instead, this wave of migration seems to have owed more to the high level of technology and organization of the emigrating population and the correspondingly less developed state of the native Slavic population (the Wends) in the zone of immigration. Moreover, the settled lands presented extremely favorable conditions to farmers and the distances were fairly short. The German immigrants had plows, axes, and tools that allowed them to deforest and cultivate difficult land. The Slavs hunted and fished and practiced an itinerant agriculture that entailed the abandonment of fields once their fertility was exhausted. The circumstances and characteristics of the migration, organized and planned by the clergy and nobility, by the chivalric Orders (Templar and Teutonic Knights), and by the great religious orders (Cistercians, Premonstratensians) are as follows. First, the leaders were able to pick and choose specific lands – uncultivated ones in this case – to measure, divide, and monitor the availability of water and risk of flooding. They also had capital to invest, necessary to sustain the emigrants on their journey, keep them fed until the harvest, and provide them with seeds, tools, and fundamental resources. The organization of the migration required middlemen to administer relations between the founding lords and the peasants, and so there emerged the figure of the migration agent who displayed all the characteristics of an entrepreneur.

This capacity to organize and distribute resources entailed assignment to the average family of a farm (*hufe*) of roughly 20 hectares (either the small 17 hectare Flemish farm or the larger 24 hectare Frankish one) and the establishment of villages of 200–300 people (isolated houses were the exception). Moreover, the land was free from feudal bonds far into the future and could be bequeathed, sold, or abandoned.

These favorable conditions, and the need to actively recruit participants, suggests that the supply of available land exceeded the demand:

The great extension of the movement is only explained by the fact that colonists bred colonists; for all over the world new settlers have big families. Migration from Old Germany in many cases slackened early. Conditions of tenure in the colonized areas also encouraged this colonization by colonists' families. Law or custom favoured the undivided inheritance of peasant holdings; so there were many younger sons without land.[11]

If we follow this theory, the idea of a population driven to leave its homeland solely because of the pressure of strong demographic growth (growth that did indeed exist) begins to lose ground. Rather, this process of migration appears to be self-generating, encouraged by the abundance of available land and the technological and organizational superiority of the colonists, as compared to the sparsely settled, agriculturally less developed native population. The opportunity to exchange a small farm in one's native land for a couple of dozen hectares must have been attractive. The favorable conditions encountered by the first migrants in turn provoked strong demographic growth, and so triggered successive waves of migration. In this way, the process of colonization did not require large-scale movements across long distances, but instead depended on a steady, continuous march led by generations of the offspring of colonists.

We can then describe the *Drang nach Osten* as a slow wave of progress – almost 1,000 kilometers West to East in three centuries – conceptually analogous to the spread of agriculture from the Middle East to the British Isles several millennia before. However, the latter migration differed in the way it was planned and organized, and also in that the territories that were occupied in the process of migration were not deserted, but populated by semi-nomadic Slavs. Finally, the economy, technology, culture, and society were profoundly different.

We can find characteristics similar to this wave of progress even during the peak of the Industrial Revolution: for example, in the gradual colonization of the American continent that progressed during the nineteenth century across the Mississippi River and westward to the Pacific Ocean. The shift of the "frontier" toward the west occurred for numerous reasons: political (the acquisition of new territories such as Louisiana, Texas, and California), legislative (the Homestead Act of 1862 which bestowed free land on colonists willing to improve it), technological (the 1869 completion of the transcontinental railroad), and the chance of personal gain (placer deposits of gold were discovered in California in 1849). It was a migration begun by fur trappers, miners, and ranchers, but whose driving force was made up of pioneering farmers. They were sustained by forces similar to those that sustained waves of migration in the past: the occupation of unoccupied or sparsely occupied territories by groups of prolific, agrarian families who, in turn, contributed to subsequent migrations. One well-received theory attributes the ample dimension and high rates of childbirth among the families of farmers and landowners in the nineteenth century to the greater availability of land and the low cost of providing for their children.[12] The frontier did not grow thanks to an influx of new migrants from the east – the costs of travel, acquiring and preparing land, buying tools and materials, and building a home were too high for the common worker – but thanks to the reproductive capacity of the already settled families.[13] This world, however, was a very different one from those we have considered above, and the wave of settlement was fed by migration from Europe and by industrialization, forces that rapidly destroyed the pre-existing economic order.

At just about the same time, the settling of Asiatic Russia was under way, led by a wave of peasant families crossing the Urals and consisting of 4.5 million people, more than 1 million of whom were political prisoners. It took place between the liberation of the serfs in 1861 and World War I.[14] In this case, too, we can detect traces of a wave of progress that pushed the frontier eastward, crossing the Urals, occupying Siberia and the steppes, and moving onward to the most distant eastern shores of Asia. It was pushed along by the availability of land and a high level of natural increase. We refer, though, only to "traces," as Czarist policies that sought to control and organize population movement heavily influenced the migration that was also responding to natural forces.

Similarly, the wave paradigm appears to fit the populating of Manchuria following the Manchu dynasty's conquest of China. Chinese immigration into these vast open territories, initially forbidden and then permitted, greatly intensified during the nineteenth century and counteracted the increasing pressure of Russian migration into the regions of the Usuri and Amur Rivers. The population, estimated at little more than a million in 1787, tripled by 1850 and increased sixfold between 1850 and 1904 as a result of immigration pressure from densely populated and impoverished northern China. The majority of these immigrants were peasants who produced wheat, millet, corn, and soybeans. They fed a flow of migration that reached flood stage in the 1920s with completion of the Peking–Mukden railroad.[15]

– 2 –
Selection and Reproduction
The Settler Effect

The slow and gradual wave-like migration typical of agricultural societies in unpopulated areas had two primary features. The first was the ability to move and adapt to a wide range of environments, including surprisingly challenging ones. The ability of a population to adapt was undoubtedly tied to the sum of communal experience and knowledge and the possession of technology and material resources: the greater a group's overall resources, the greater its ability to make the most of new lands. The second feature was the ability for those families and settlements at the front of the wave to generate a demographic surplus adequate to generate further expansion. Both of these features would come to define the ways in which potential migrants were selected. There is historical evidence that those people who chose to migrate were not a random sample of the general population, but had instead certain defining characteristics. Age, health, strength, stamina, and a willingness to try new things are characteristics that often set migrants apart from those who stay put. These are conjectures, however, as data on prehistoric peoples are non-existent, and historical evidence is limited. That which does exist we employ below.

As a first case, we shall look at the capacity for growth of migrant groups arriving in populated territories. In these examples, migrants come into contact with native populations and so are in competition with them for both natural resources and social or political dominance. The effects of this sort of immigration are particularly evident when the migrant population, for a variety of different reasons, does not mix with the native one. Those reasons might include settlement in isolated areas or intentional separation due to religious, cultural, or political differences. Different reproductive capacities produce changes in the numerical relationships between groups. In general, the reproductive fitness of a group is expressed by the numerical relationship between one generation and that preceding it. If the ratio between the two groups is close to one, the population does not change. If the ratio is above or below one, the population either grows or shrinks. Reproductive fitness is simply a combination of the tendency to have children and the ability to ensure their survival. History is full of examples of migrant and native populations with different reproductive capacities, not unlike the situation in nature when a species migrates into a new territory and competes with the native species for available resources. One of the species might eliminate the other, or they may find a quantitative balance. If the migrant group possesses greater technology or knowledge, it may achieve better living conditions at the expense of the native population; or the exact opposite can occur. The quantitative success or failure of an immigrant group is inextricably linked to the level of reproductive fitness a group can achieve and maintain over time. In this case we are considering an abstract situation in which there is no mixing between migrants and natives.

A real-world example of this process can be found in the history of the Americas over the last 500 years and the consequences of contact with Europe and Africa. Indeed, it provides an inexhaustible source of demographic, social, and cultural experiences observable on a continental scale, over both the long term and the short term, and offering examples of the interactions between different populations.

Indios, Europeans, and Africans, the latter almost all forced into slavery, experienced very different quantitative outcomes. Europeans expanded rapidly, particularly in certain parts of the continent where abundant resources and favorable climate led to higher rates of both survival and birth. Their survival benefitted from abundant food, sparse settlement (which was less conducive to the spread of infectious diseases), and a sort of natural selection exercised by the challenges of transoceanic voyage. Birth rates also rose, as the widespread availability of material resources and open space freed individuals from the strict social constraints on reproduction that in Europe encouraged celibacy and relatively late marriage and childbearing. In other words, the reproductive fitness of the migrant groups was strengthened in their new environments, the numerical results of which we shall discuss shortly. For the native populations, quite the opposite occurred. The Indios were stripped of their ability to govern themselves and to own land: their labor was partially confiscated and their traditional ways of life changed or disrupted. With the Europeans came viruses – smallpox, measles, scarlet fever – against which the natives lacked immunity and which threatened their very existence. Territorial relocation, economic disruption, and forced entry into their genetic pool on the part of the Europeans greatly lowered native birth rates. Their reproductive fitness was severely impaired, and for several generations they suffered a dramatic population decline. In competition with the new arrivals, they were the losers. The fate that awaited the Africans, millions of whom were transported to America as slaves, was still worse. The changes in climate, the grueling labor, and the conditions associated with slavery meant their rate of survival was universally very low. Birth rates too were lowered for a variety of reasons, in particular, the obstacles that slave owners put in the way of marriage and the establishment of families among slaves: it was less useful to invest in reproduction than to simply purchase new slaves as they arrived from Africa.[1]

Though America was 100 percent Native American in the year 1500, three centuries later Europeans and Africans constituted the vast majority.[2] Here we might try a simple calculation, albeit a rough one given the modest amount of quantitative data available to historians. For Africans and Europeans, we will use two related variables: P (population) and I (immigration). The first variable (P) consists of the size of the respective population around the year 1800, based on censuses, estimates, and other data. The second variable (I) is the cumulative net population flow (so subtracting returns) during the years 1500–1800. In addition, P (i.e., the Europeans or Africans living in America in 1800) is itself the product of two components. The first is the flow of immigration that occurred during the three centuries taken into consideration (I). The second is the reproductive fitness, or growth, of populations of African and European immigrants during the period. Reproductive fitness (F) is nothing more than the combination of survival and birth rate. Therefore, if $P = I \times F$, it follows that:

$$F = P : I$$

The rough estimate of reproductive fitness is given by the relation between the final population count and the cumulative (net) number of immigrants, assuming that one can estimate these quantities.[3] In 1800, the number of Americans of European descent was about 8 million: 4.5 million in North America and 3.5 million Central and South America (of which 2.5 million in the Hispanic colonies and 1 million in Portuguese Brazil). These 8 million were the descendants of a net flow of immigrants over three centuries of roughly 2.3 million people. Their fitness then was equal to 8/2.3 = 3.5.

On its own, this number is fairly abstract and does not reveal much. But it speaks volumes when compared with the same calculation for the African immigrant population. In 1800, the number of African immigrants in the Americas was roughly 5.6 million. The number of Africans who were forcibly transported in slave ships over the three preceding centuries was around 7.2 million. Fitness for the African population (5.6/7.2 = 0.8) was not only less than a fourth of that of the Europeans, but less than one, and so a sign of negative growth. In other words, during those three centuries, the African population in America would have entirely disappeared had it not been reinforced by the constant arrival of new slaves from Africa.

These simple calculations demonstrate the hugely variable experiences of different immigrant populations, variation that occurred within the European and African ethnic groups as well. The fitness value was around 7.2 for French Canadians, 4.7 for the English in North America, 3.1 for the Spanish in Latin America, and 2.0 for the Portuguese in Brazil. We should treat these figures with caution, as there are surely errors in both the basic data and the calculations, not to mention the varying importance of racial mixing. However, we can state with confidence that these differences were not owing to differences in the sending populations – the demographic regimes and models of growth had essentially leveled out in Europe, and the discrepancies there were different from those found in America – but instead can be largely attributed to the conditions encountered in the New World. Differential mortality derived from climatic and environmental changes, from the prevalence of certain diseases, and from the intensity of epidemic cycles. Likely also important was the fact that the Europeans in North America were mostly farmers, for whom large families and an abundance of manpower were advantageous, while the Europeans in Latin America were predominantly city-dwellers, merchants, administrators, artisans, and proprietors, groups less likely to have large families. In any case, there was a notable disparity between the fitness of these different populations.

Among the Africans, the situation was dramatically different: in the Caribbean, where nearly 4 million slaves were brought between 1500 and 1800, there were only 1.7 million people of African descent in 1800 (giving the Afro-Caribbeans a fitness value of 0.4), while 2.3 million slaves were shipped to Brazil, but the population in 1800 (black and mulatto) was less than 2 million (a fitness value of 0.9). Only in North America (fitness value of 2.9) and Spanish America (1.2) – which together received only one slave ship in seven of those bound for the New World – was the situation better.

It is worth focusing momentarily on the case of French immigrants along the St Lawrence Seaway in Quebec in the seventeenth century to more clearly understand the advantages that intercontinental travel might exercise on the size of a population. Thanks to the careful precision with which French Canadian parish priests recorded baptisms, marriages, and burials, scholars have managed to reconstruct with great accuracy the genealogy of the pioneers over their first two centuries in North America, and compare their history with that of Normandy and Brittany whence they came.[4] The first pioneers had a higher rate of survival than their countrymen in Europe, presumably tied to the greater availability of food, the slower diffusion of transmissible diseases in the vast and largely unpopulated St Lawrence River valley, and the more robust constitution required for migration. In addition, the French Canadians married earlier and had more children and larger families. And this reproductive fitness did not only characterize the first generation of pioneers, but continued with their descendants. The ways of life of the new American society, the immense amounts of available land, and its extensive cultivation favored a high investment in reproduction. Each pioneer couple had, on average, 6.3 children, 4.2 of whom reached adulthood and married. The base immigrant population doubled in less than 30 years. Moreover, the pioneer's four surviving children would go on to have an average of 28 children between them, giving each pioneer 34 offspring between children and grandchildren. One pioneer in three had over 50 descendants. Adam Smith was most certainly correct in his observation, in reference to the rapid demographic growth of North America, that: "The value of children is the greatest of all encouragements to marriage."[5] One other point is worth noting: between 1608 and 1700 the number of French immigrants who arrived, and stayed, in Canada was 4,669. Subsequently, immigration slowed down significantly, and the population grew almost exclusively thanks to the natural growth of that early group. Indeed, it is estimated that those few thousand original settlers from the seventeenth century are the progenitors of roughly two thirds of the nearly 7 million French Canadians alive today. Concurrent with the success of the French was the decline of the indigenous populations (Algonquin, Iroquois, Hurons), pushed out of their homelands by foreigners, and struck down by new diseases.

The French Canadian case is the best-documented example of a story that has been repeated in different continents and different centuries. Europeans controlled sources of energy (horses and other draft animals, sailing ships) and technology (iron, steel tools, weapons, wheels, and explosives). They were protected by better clothing and better shelters, and functioned well in cold and temperate climates. Finally, the animals they brought with them (horses, cows, goats, sheep, pigs) adapted to the new environment with stunning ease, as did their plants and seeds. A small number of immigrants exercised a powerful foundation effect – remarkably so in the case of the French Canadians – establishing large and well-rooted populations.

The migration process – barring cases involving the transfer of an entire population – presumably entails a degree of natural selection (biophysical, psychological, social): the migrant population will differ from those who remain behind. Given the nearly infinite variety of migrations, it would be pointless to enumerate examples. It is, however, reasonable to assume that the selection effect was transitory, reflected in the migrants but not their descendants. This is almost certainly the case for most of the social traits acquired throughout one's lifetime; and while some characteristics, a trade, for example, may be passed from parent to child, it is unlikely that they will be maintained for generations. Certain physical and biological characteristics are almost certainly selected for in migration. For example, an arduous journey over long and difficult distances, by sea or by land, naturally weeds out the weakest or sickest or least skilled members of a group. Or the trauma of adapting to a new environment will exclude those members of a group least open to change.

Conscription exams conducted by Italian consular officials for Italian immigrants in the US provide an interesting example. Judgments that individual applicants did not meet the minimum physical requirements for conscription were relatively rare among the young men examined in the US as compared to those examined in Italy, even though the military physicians were notoriously more likely to offer exemptions to the immigrant group.[6] Apparently migration selected the most fit. If a comparison were to be made between the sons of the immigrants and their peers in Italy, it is unlikely any large differences would be found. Another test, in this case indirect, comes from the comparison of survivorship between European populations and populations of European origin. From the end of the nineteenth century to the middle of the twentieth, New Zealand and Australia enjoyed better longevity than the most advanced European countries, for example, those of Scandinavia. With regard to New Zealand – which enjoyed the highest-recorded life expectancy between 1876 and 1930 – here is the explanation provided by Jacques Vallin and France Meslé:

The rapid growth of the non-Maori population was achieved mainly through large-scale immigration, which brought in new settlers who were strongly selected by the difficulties of acquiring the means to emigrate from Europe and surviving the long voyage. The health conditions of the initial European settlers were exceptionally favored by that selection.[7]

This effect gradually faded as the population of New Zealand grew; and it eventually lost its number one spot.

Fertility behavior also reveals the rapid decrease of natural selection effects. In the previous chapter, we suggested that agricultural families comprising the migratory "wave of progress" enjoyed a high rate of reproduction, allowing them to grow fast enough to fuel continued expansion, and we can cite multiple examples: from the German *Drang nach Osten* to the westward movement of the American frontier in the nineteenth century. Moreover, in agriculture-based economies with large amounts of available land, elevated fertility was an advantage. But as we enter the contemporary era, it is doubtful that a high birth rate remained favorable. First of all, the costs of reproduction grew as the benefits shrank, and a lower equilibrium was struck. Consider once again Italian migration to America. Italian immigrant women came primarily from the countryside of southern Italy and, as measured in the US census at the beginning of the twentieth century, differed notably from other (white) women born in America: they married at a younger age and with greater frequency (few remained unmarried); and they had more children and were far less likely to be without children at the end of their childbearing years. These behaviors, symptomatic of their elevated reproductive fitness, may in part be attributed to selection factors of migration. In any case, these women differed not only from the native population at their point of arrival, but also from the population they left behind (in this case that of rural southern Italy). This "reproductive advantage," however, was of little use in the new urban and industrial societies where these women found themselves. Confirming the observation that a chief characteristic of most immigrant groups is their adaptability, the child-bearing habits of these Italian women changed rapidly. For example, in 1920, the median number of children brought into the world by women born in Italy was almost exactly double that of (white) women born in the United States: 6.34 versus 3.15. The gap, however, shrank rapidly, and already in 1936 the number of children born to women of Italian origin was below that of American women: 2.08 versus 2.14.[8] It goes without saying that more accurate and detailed information would be required to better quantify this phenomenon, but alas, that information is unavailable. Nonetheless, this striking example of mutation-adaptation is just one of many that can be drawn from the history of migration in the contemporary world.[9]

And today? What are the reproductive habits of foreign immigrants in new countries, especially those coming from regions of high or very high fertility? Is there the possibility of a "displacement" of the native population because of the uncontrolled growth of the immigrant population? Or from another point of view: can an immigrant population, by virtue of its propensity to bear children, mitigate or eliminate the birth deficit suffered by a native population? These questions are complex but not intractable. We should first make a distinction between the life cycle (and reproductive cycle) experience of first-generation immigrants before leaving their country of origin and after arriving at their new destination. In those two contexts, they may encounter two radically different environments and so behave in dissimilar ways. Then we need to consider the behavior of subsequent generations: whether the descendants of immigrants begin to converge to – or diverge from – the behavior and social practices of the native population. We should add that present-day differences in survivorship are relatively small and so bear little on reproductive fitness; they can often be disregarded. In the American experience, similar to that of many other immigrant nations, the descendants of the great European migration, toward the middle of the last century, were characterized by reproductive behavior that was indistinguishable from that of the native population; the divergent habits of their parents and grandparents had practically disappeared. The same can be said for the migrations of non-Europeans that began in the middle of the twentieth century. Second- or third-generation families of Asian, Latino, and Caribbean descent did not retain the reproductive behaviors of their ancestors. In the course of about a generation, the convergence of reproductive models is, in general, guaranteed.

For the first generation of immigrants, recent European experience suggests that natural selection favors the migration of women with more moderate reproductive behavior relative to their place of origin. At the end of their reproductive period, they seem to have given birth to a bit over two children per woman, slightly more than the average in their country of destination, but not enough to cause any significant spike in the population. In France (1991–8), the average number of children born to women who had migrated from the Maghreb was 2.8 (versus 3.3 in their home countries); for those coming from the rest of Africa it was 2.9 (versus 5.9); and for those from Asia it was 1.8 (versus 2.9). In Lombardy, data on births in 2008 to women of non-European descent put the number at 2.1, certainly higher than the 1.3 children born to Italian women, but given the relatively small number of immigrant women, not sufficient to have any significant impact on the general level of reproduction.[10]

Over the last couple of centuries, the reproductive advantage of first-generation immigrants over the native population has been considerable. However, the scale of this phenomenon is shrinking, in part due to the widespread availability of birth control in countries of origin, but also because the process of migration tends to select individuals who are more suited to the destination societies and so characterized by more moderate fertility. The reproductive advantage of succeeding generations is instead almost zero, and the immigrant part of a population tends to grow at the same rate as the natives.

Comparing two immigrant populations: the roughly 650,000 Italian women of all ages living in the United States in 1917 (the first year for which this information is available) gave birth to 127,000 children.[11] Almost a century later, in 2008, the roughly 2 million foreign women living in Italy (three times the previous number of Italian women in the United States) gave birth to 84,000 children – one child for every five women then; one child for every 25 women today.

– 3 –

Organized Migrations

As we have already seen, waves of expansion occur slowly and gradually and require a high degree of individual initiative. The advantage, or perceived advantage, of new settlements encouraged groups to migrate and others to follow them and travel to new lands. With the rise of complex political entities and of states, individual initiative was seconded by efforts to guide, regulate, and organize migration. As territories came under forms of sovereign rule, regulations regarding citizenship were created and borders were drawn. Knowledge of the land, including more remote areas, grew and was consolidated into an ever more precise cartography. Migration policies were born, of which there are numerous historical examples interesting to compare both in terms of implementation and outcome. Mobility, an essential component of human capital, encountered new limitations beyond those imposed by environmental constraints.

Organized migrations are of course not restricted to the modern era. For example, the foundation of Greek settlements around the Mediterranean between the eighth and the sixth centuries BCE, pushed by demographic growth and the limited availability of land, followed an organizational model. The process of migrating to, settling, and founding these colonies – *apoikoi* – was carried out under the guidance of an assigned leader – *oikistes* – who employed specific criteria to select those migrants who would maximize the success of the colonies. And so a dense network of settlements came to dot the coastlines of the Black Sea, Anatolia, and northern Africa all the way to the Iberian Peninsula.

In the following chapters, we will briefly sketch out the great migratory paths of the modern era. Here, instead, we ask a basic question: in what way and to what extent do politics affect the outcome of migration? What is their effect on the fitness of a migrant group, or on their social and economic success? While we cannot provide exhaustive answers to such complex and significant questions, we can make a first attempt by assessing the success or failure of immigrants in demographic terms.

A paradigmatic example can be drawn from the distant past. The expansion of Incan government over the peoples of the Andes took place in a relatively short span of time and across a vast expanse of land, environments ranging from coastal regions to populous highlands 4,000 meters above sea level. Incan policy included the settlement of groups of colonists (*mitima*) in regions far from the center of the empire in order to consolidate conquered lands, spread Incan culture, and focus on specialized production.[1] Moreover, special attention was paid to ensuring environmental and ecological compatibility, in order to not compromise the survival of the immigrant groups. This same sort of concern was not shown by the Spaniards, at least in the first years of the *Conquista*, as they only gradually came to recognize the widespread suffering inflicted on populations hastily transplanted from the highlands to the lower torrid regions, and vice versa. In cases such as these, migration greatly compromised the fitness of the population, lowering their survival rate.

The history of organized migration is a complex one. In many cases, the long-lasting effects of these undertakings were beneficial, sometimes remarkably so, and might exercise a "foundation effect." In other cases, the circumstances surrounding a geographical population transfer proved disastrous. This is a good metric by which to judge the effects of migratory politics. In the first chapter, we discussed the eastward wave of German progress beyond the Elbe, Oder, and Vistula Rivers, and the significant organizational roles played by the nobility, the Church, and the chivalric Orders. We can reasonably ascribe part of the overall success of these migrations – the rise of efficient agriculture and the formation of an effective network of settlement – to these forces. The circumstances and characteristics of the migration were carefully planned from the outset: fertile and arable land fit for colonizing was chosen in advance and was then evenly distributed among the colonists. The colonists were also provided with seed, livestock, building materials, and tools to ensure their survival. "The German immigrants were equipped with the heavy, wheeled plough with coulter and mouldboard and they had heavy felling axes with which they could clear the thicker forests in order to cultivate the heavier soils."[2] A manager or "chief settler" of sorts acted as an intermediary between the capitalists and the peasants and supervised the migrations. There may also have been a filtering mechanism to select families, especially those that provided maximum labor. This capacity for planning and organization made possible the allocation of ample farmlands to the average family and the construction of villages which housed several dozen families. As we have already seen, the land remained the property of those who worked it and could be passed down through generations, sold off, or abandoned. And since the system of non-partitive inheritance prevailed, the younger siblings remained without land and so were forced to migrate yet again.[3] Judging from the growth of the Germanic population east of the border of the Carolingian Empire during the following centuries, there is little doubt that this migration was a success, a demographic success that reflected the foresight of those political leaders who embarked on such a massive migratory undertaking.

In the modern era, the monarchies of Europe frequently resorted to organized migrations; it was an established tenet of mercantilist philosophy that a large and rapidly growing population was one of the pillars of a great nation. Schumpeter observed that according to the mercantilists: "a numerous and increasing population was the most important *symptom* of wealth; it was the chief *cause* of wealth; it *was* wealth itself – the greatest asset for any nation to have," and that opinion dominated until the second half of the eighteenth century.[4] Two important factors motivated migratory choices. The first was economic in nature and focused on the exploitation of uncultivated lands in sparsely populated areas, or areas left depopulated by the crisis of the seventeenth century. The second was political and strategic, and consisted of fortifying border areas adjacent to hostile or potentially aggressive neighbors. Occasionally, these two factors overlapped, particularly on the eastern and southern borders of the Austrian and Russian Empires.

A successful example, though not without its problems, is the German migration promoted by Catherine II shortly after her ascension to the imperial throne in 1762. The principal motives behind this migration were twofold. The first goal was to modernize the backward system of Russian agriculture through an influx of peasants capable of putting into practice more modern techniques. The second was to create a sort of buffer zone in the depopulated areas between the Russians and the semi-nomadic peoples to the east of the lower Volga. To this end, in December 1762 a first Royal Manifesto was issued, translated into several languages, and distributed by the agents of the Crown in various European countries. The manifesto outlined the various benefits and privileges to be bestowed on those who chose to emigrate to Russia. These included free transport, cash payments, free land, freedom of religion and to build churches, administrative autonomy, 10-year interest-free loans to build homes and buy tools, 30-year exemption from taxes, and perpetual exemption from military service. The immigrants were also guaranteed the right to return to their country of origin. At first the size of the land grants was not specified, but it was described in a subsequent decree and set at around 80 acres (32 hectares, slightly larger than the land assigned five or six centuries before to the principal colonists of the *Drang nach Osten*). Though the conditions were attractive to the impoverished populations of Germany, who had been particularly hard hit by the recently concluded Seven Years War, the initial turnout was disappointing. A second manifesto was issued in July of the following year, and a chancellery was established to manage the settlement of the foreign migrants. This second proclamation was more successful than the first, thanks in part to the work of an army of well-paid recruitment agents dispersed throughout Europe. Certain countries, such as Austria, prohibited distribution of the manifesto, while others were geographically too remote. But the response among the peoples of western and southern Germany and the free cities of the Holy Roman Empire was significant, and a wave of immigrants made their way to the ports of Lübeck and Hamburg. From there, they sailed to St Petersburg whence they were transported overland to their destinations along the banks of the lower Volga.

Between 1763 and 1767, the year when the German princes put an end to the exodus, roughly 30,000 migrants, consisting primarily of young families, migrated to the banks of the Volga and the Karaman. They founded 104 settlements (composed of a few dozen families each), which grew more numerous as the population increased. However, not everything went according to plan. Among the migrants, some were not well suited to the colonists' life, and the settlements suffered the devastation of Pugachev's rebellion in 1774.[5] Despite this setback, the settlements prospered both socially and demographically without any supplementary migrations (apart from a small group of Mennonites) for over a century. In 1871, Czar Alexander II revoked the exemption from military service, and there followed a wave of migration to the United States that lasted until 1917. The Imperial Census of 1897, which accurately recorded linguistic and religious minorities, counted 1.312 million Germans in "European Russia" (excluding the Polish and Caucasian provinces), many of whom were settled in the Baltic and western regions and in the Crimea. In the remote Volga region, the censors counted over a third of the total German population (471,843, with 224,336 in Samara, 166,528 in Saratov, and 80,979 in Ekaterinoslav).

In the span of 130 years, the initial group of settlers had multiplied by 16, doubling every generation. It was an extraordinary demographic "success" and a dramatic example of the "foundation effect." As is well known, this success led eventually to political disaster: in 1924 the Volga colonies became one of the autonomous republics (the Volga German ASSR) of the Soviet Union. The republic was dissolved in 1941 by Stalin, and its inhabitants were sent to Siberia. Those who survived chose not to return to the region, and emigrated to Germany after 1980, taking advantage of the "law of return."

The eighteenth century was filled with attempts at organized colonization, and several ended in disaster. The Tuscan Maremma was devastated in 1552 by the imperial troops sent by Cosimo I in an attempt to take control of Siena. Much of the population fled, and land reclamation projects were abandoned as the area deteriorated quickly and malaria spread throughout the region. Already in 1560, Cosimo I attempted to repopulate the region by transplanting about 200 families, mainly from Lombardy. A subsequent attempt was made a century later with a group of Morean Greeks, coaxed into leaving their homes with the promise of privileges and subsidies. The long-term outcome of these two migrations is not known, but partial evidence relating to the Lombard group suggests a devastating mortality rate of 10 percent in the first 18 months.

More is known about an ambitious project conceived by Francesco II, the first Grand Duke of Lorraine, in 1739:

> The approach was much like that of Cosimo I. A crier from the Grand Duke was sent to Lorraine with a declaration in French and German that announced the advantages offered to the colonists, advantages set out in subsequent documents. Each family was to receive a tract of land for planting grain together with other lots for grape vines, olive trees, and a vegetable garden; two oxen; a milk cow; and two goats for which no repayment was required during the first six years. They would also receive grain for planting, tools, two pounds and four ounces of bread per person per day until the harvest, four *soldi* per day for each family member regardless of age or sex, and exemption from taxes for twenty years.[6]

The announcement seems to have received a positive and rapid response which surprised the authorities; the first families began arriving in the summer of 1739 and were housed temporarily in Florence, Prato, and Pisa before being transferred to the Maremma in 1743. The precise number of colonists that arrived in Tuscany is unknown – perhaps 5,000 – as many deserted before they could be relocated permanently to the Sovana and Massa districts. Only a few years after the final settling, the colony was already on the verge of extinction, having lost a large part of its initial stock. The rapid decline owed as much to abandonment as to high mortality, a situation of which the migration authorities were well aware: hygienic conditions were poor, housing inadequate, food distribution hampered by corruption, and malaria widespread. In short, the combination of poor planning, an unhealthy region, and malaria all but guaranteed failure.

During the 1760s, under Charles III, Pablo de Olavide directed the migration of thousands of German immigrants to settle the Sierra Morena in Andalusia. This undertaking was inspired by the Enlightenment idea that a new colony would flourish because freed of the negative elements understood to have caused the decline of Spanish agriculture:

> The reorganization of agriculture would exclude the Mesta and their practice of transhumant livestock raising. Nor would the land be allowed to fall into the hands of a few large holders. The clergy would be prevented from exercising its pernicious influence, and men of letters and petty-foggers would also be excluded except for physicians and the necessary administrators. Various causes contributed to the relative failure of the experiment – technical problems relating to the colonization process, political and financial obstacles, and the difficulties of assimilation experienced by the foreign colonists – though ultimately the sole and primary cause may have been improvisation.[7]

Chapter 4 will explore planned migrations in other parts of Europe and some also in America. To cite one New World example, King John V of Portugal issued an edict on August 9, 1747, outlining an ambitious plan to colonize the island of Santa Catarina and the adjacent Brazilian mainland with 4,000 families from the Azores and Madeira. The colonists were provided with free passage; adequate shares of flour, corn, and other foodstuffs for the first year; a "quarter of a league" of land for each family; seed and tools; as well as two cows and a mare. Every community would also receive 4 bulls and 2 stallions. Supplies were allotted for the building of communities that would support up to 60 families.[8] We were unable, however, to locate any documents describing the outcome of the plan.

These examples range from events that occurred over very long periods of time – the German *Drang nach Osten* – to those that lasted only a few years and ended in complete failure. The fact is that the outcome of migratory processes cannot be reduced to simple measures of departures and arrivals. Their consequences only emerge over time, often a very long time, and are affected by the initial "choices" made, whether political or not. Organization can influence the "fitness" of a migrant group, imposing selection criteria, providing resources, and choosing both the sending region and the destination. In instances such as these, we are no longer considering a process of self-selection, as in the case of the "waves of progress," where mistakes are attributable to the migrants themselves. The combination of selection criteria can lead to contrasting results: success as in the Volga colonies, or failure as in the Maremma and Andalusia. The privileges bestowed upon the migrants were similar, but the differences lay in planning, the choice of areas for settlement, the availability of space, competition with native populations, and maybe even the civil liberties granted to the migrants. Political mistakes were paid for by the migrants and might lead to failure of the migratory initiative. And so it went for the first organized migration to the New World when a new governor was sent to Hispaniola following the removal of Columbus and his brothers as rulers of the island. Ovando arrived in Santo Domingo on April 15, 1502, leading a fleet of 32 ships with 2,500 passengers. The selection of migrants, however, proved to be a failure: only the wealthy could afford passage; the rest were soldiers, servants, artisans, and functionaries. According to Las Casas, roughly 1,000 headed for the recently discovered gold deposits in the nearby hills:

> Reaching the deposits, seeing as gold does not grow on trees and is instead buried beneath the ground, they commenced to dig for it in the earth, without knowledge or experience of how gold is found in veins or deposits, and soon they became tired of digging. Those men had no experience of digging, and so it came to pass that more than 1,000 of the 2,500 came to die, and 500 more, in a state of great distress and hunger, fell ill. And this was the fate that befell all those who came seeking gold in the New World.[9]

In short, a rough start for the new colony, not only due to the lack of women but because a great many of the men participating in the expensive venture were not suited to the life that awaited them. The lure of gold was disastrous for the migrants. The lure of steel, instead, proved more useful: the missionaries sent to the Americas knew this well as they coaxed Indian tribes into rejecting their nomadic lifestyles and traveling sometimes hundreds of miles to live in missionary communities. The gift of a steel ax, which in comparison with those made of stone, could fell a tree in a twentieth of the time, was an irresistible incentive as it decreased workloads and improved the quality of life.

Finally, a demographic consideration serves to reinforce a point made in the previous chapter, namely, that the "foundation effect" of migrations prior to the nineteenth century, when survival rates were universally low and resources and knowledge in short supply, can be ascribed mainly to fertility. On the other hand, in the absence of birth control (a modern invention), the differences in birth rates can be attributed primarily to age at marriage, or onset of the reproductive life cycle, and the degree to which some individuals are excluded from marriage and reproduction. Migrations carried out in areas with abundant natural resources and arable land presented good prospects for future generations and led to early marriages and a high birth rate.

We have already examined several interesting historical cases, but let us close with one final example from the Jewish diaspora that began in the sixteenth century. This was not a planned migration, as the driving force behind the diaspora was flight from danger and not the prospect of new lands to settle. Sergio Della Pergola writes:

> Around 1900, the Jewish community in Eastern Europe, along with their descendants overseas, totaled about 7.5 million; in Italy instead there were about 43,000 Jews. And yet at the end of the fifteenth century, these two groups were similar in size (20–50,000 people).[10]

Behind this surprising numerical comparison lay vastly different demographic systems: a balance between births and deaths and an absence of growth in Italy, versus a high rate of death and an even higher rate of birth in the East, the latter supported by social norms and a tight family structure. How much of this difference can be ascribed to the tight spatial constraints to which Jews were subjected in the Italian ghettos versus the relative freedom of movement and the vastness of Eastern Europe that was available to the Ashkenazim?

– 4 –

Three Centuries

1500–1800

Humans have legs. The ability and tendency to move from place to place is part of human nature and a valuable prerogative for adaptation and bettering the human condition. For hunter-gatherers, it was a vital tool for survival; for agriculturalists, it aided in better exploiting territorial possibilities and for exchanging the goods of the earth; and for merchants, it was a frequent necessity. The modern history of Europe, till the dawn of the Industrial Revolution, was characterized by increased mobility over distances ranging from short to very long. A consistent flow of transoceanic migration began after 1500. Europe, which in previous centuries had been a destination for immigration, became instead a source of emigration. Once an importer of human resources, it became an exporter; and the direction of that flow changed once again in the second half of the twentieth century. The fact is that net loss to migration between 1500 and 1800 was modest: average migration to the Americas (see chapter 2) did not exceed 1 million per century,[1] not much for a continent that counted 100 million inhabitants at the beginning of that period and double that at the end. Yet it was sufficient to impose new languages, culture, religion, and institutions on a vast continent. Within Europe itself, medium- and short-range mobility improved; cities grew and so too did the migration between country and city; labor markets expanded to embrace transnational regions; and settlement migration filled the lesser-populated parts of Eastern Europe.

Objective factors improved the conditions for human mobility: the increased availability of energy (even before the spread of the steam engine) combined with technological innovations to improve infrastructure (roads, bridges, canals, and ports). It has been calculated that by the mid-eighteenth century, per capita energy consumption in Europe amounted to about 14–15,000 calories per day, half consisting of thermal energy (from the burning of wood) and half mechanical (derived from both human and animal sources), and so potentially used for hauling and travel. Water and wind contributed little (perhaps 1 percent of the total).[2] The contribution of human energy to this total was modest, rarely more than 2,500 kcal per day. Traveling 10 kilometers on foot with a 10 kg pack containing provisions, tools, and clothing cost around 200 calories, and imposed an objective limit on the mobility of populations that not infrequently found themselves at the limits of subsistence.[3] The availability of beasts of burden multiplied available energy: among the populations of Central and Northern Europe, the availability of a work animal was the norm and average consumption may have reached 20,000 calories per capita per day; that figure, however, may have declined to 5,000 for a peasant in the Mediterranean regions, who often lacked cow, donkey, or horse. From the late Middle Ages to the eve of the Industrial Revolution, caloric consumption presumably increased, especially because of the more widespread and efficient use of animal energy. That mobility doubtless contributed to the greater mobility of the population.

Increased mobility was also the result of a long series of innovations and their gradual and uneven application.

Horses became more useful and efficient, thanks to a series of developments: the introduction of horseshoes, stirrups, and other refinements (including the harnessing of shoulder and chest for traction, rather than neck); the spread of the four-wheeled cart; new methods for harnessing teams of horses; the improvement of roads; the building of bridges; and the digging of canals. The growing use of internal waterways – in which Europe abounds – and the building of canals stimulated the transportation of merchandise, especially, but also of passengers.

Improvements in navigation and the better use of wind power allowed for the transoceanic transportation of goods and people. The effect was great given the small amount of total European energy consumption involved (a fraction of a percent), and it was a development largely restricted to the Atlantic powers: the great sailing ships of Portugal in the fourteenth and fifteenth centuries made longer voyages possible and so the conquest of new spaces. There were developments in the Mediterranean too, both with regard to increased capacity and new navigational techniques (lateen sails, compasses, and rudders), but the great advances came in the Atlantic: the development of advanced rigging, the transition from single-masted to triple-masted ships, and the increase in tonnage.[4] These improvements allowed for increased carrying capacity, greater security, faster travel, and lower costs. The average length of a trip between Seville and America was about five weeks, not that long if one considers that at the beginning of the twentieth century an ocean liner still took about 10 days to make the same trip. In a word, the modern era saw a notable increase in the ability of Europeans to move about.

In medieval Europe, most travel was short-range – at most a few dozen kilometers to get to a church, the market, or a fair – and accomplished for the most part on foot and with beasts of burden; the use of wheeled carts was rare and the roads might become impassable because of inclement weather. In the seventeenth and eighteenth centuries, mobility improved significantly. In England, coaches and wagons traced a dense transportation network and one vehicle might carry as many as 20 people. Leaving from London, one could arrive in Oxford (60 miles) in a day, and in York (200 miles) in four days. That network also included inns where travelers might stay.[5] Beginning in the late seventeenth century, private investment in canals and roads was great: around 1750, there were 1,000 miles of navigable canals, a figure that had quadrupled by 1820; toll roads grew even faster: the 3,400 miles of 1750 quadrupled already by just 1770.[6] In Holland, a dense network of roads, canals, and waterways supported urbanization, high labor mobility, and intensive internal migration: "Beginning in 1632, horse-drawn barges, *trekschuiten*, maintained regularly scheduled passenger services on routes that eventually blanketed Holland and stretched across Friesland and Groningen."[7] In 1664, on a series of internal itineraries, the Dutch traveled the equivalent of 40 million passenger-kilometers. In the century leading up to the French Revolution of 1789, investment in French roads increased by a factor of 10; by 1787, there were 53,000 kilometers of roads, and a well-run service of stagecoaches traversed the country.[8] Throughout much of Europe, investment in infrastructure increased notably over the course of the eighteenth century, though at a slower pace in those areas outside the core of industrialization. There were of course limits to that growth: horses, coaches, and boats permitted a maximum speed of about 100 kilometers per day.

Another aspect of this increased mobility was intensification of the urban fabric as the flow of population arriving from the countryside increased. The cities suffered from a chronic demographic deficit – deaths far exceeded births – and even to maintain a given population size they depended upon rural imports. Between 1500 and 1800, the urban population (living in centers with more than 10,000 inhabitants) grew almost everywhere, both in absolute terms and as a percentage of the total: from 3 to

20 percent in England and Wales, from 4 to 9 in France, from 6 to 11 in Spain, and from 12 to 14 in Italy. Between 1650 and 1750, London's population expanded by about 250,000, in spite of an equivalent increase in deaths relative to births: those figures imply a net migration (the difference between immigrants and emigrants) during that century of about half a million. The population of Amsterdam grew from 30,000 to 200,000 between 1550 and 1700, and this city was a destination for immigrants coming from Flanders, Germany, and Norway. Net migration to Rome during the eighteenth century exceeded 130,000; Naples grew from 150,000 to 280,000 in the sixteenth century and again, after the crisis of the seventeenth century, from 200,000 to 320,000 in the eighteenth; net migration was a major factor.[9]

Further testimony to increased mobility in Europe was the creation of extensive labor markets, characterized largely by seasonal and periodic work and employing mostly peasants, laborers, and smallholders seeking supplementary income. At the end of the eighteenth century, the North Sea coast, and especially Holland, received a constant influx of migrant workers for maritime work and the building of dams; the Irish went to London and East Anglia for public works and agricultural work; while the Paris basin attracted workers from the Massif Central and the Alps. Other highly mobile labor markets could be found farther south: Madrid and Castile attracted laborers for the harvest; while the coastal area from Catalonia to Provence drew laborers from the Pyrenees, the Massif Central, and the Alps. Important destinations in Italy included the Po Valley (from the Alps and the Apennines), southern Tuscany, Rome and Latium, and Corsica.[10] Most of these migrants traveled on foot, but transport via both water and land also contributed to an intense migration that counted several hundreds of thousands of workers per year who supplemented the incomes of a similar number of families and contributed in a fundamental way to the economic balance of the continent.

In the modern era, Europeans continued to engage in long-distance travel and resettlement, often across regional and national boundaries. Following the crisis of the fourteenth and fifteenth centuries – during which demographic decline led to the abandonment of much land and many villages – the movement eastward continued. In the sixteenth and seventeenth centuries, colonization of lands taken from the Slavs formed an integral part of the territorial strategy of both Prussia and Austria. Following the Thirty Years War, new German settlements were established in Pomerania with immigrants coming from Brandenburg and Silesia. The acquisition of Silesia by Frederick II of Prussia, in 1740, led to the transfer of large numbers of colonists and the Germanization of that region. It is estimated that between the last part of the seventeenth century and the end of Frederick II's reign, 430,000 colonists settled within an enlarged Prussia and so contributed to the rapid growth and further Germanization of that country. Meanwhile, German migration into Hungary also continued, estimated at about 350,000 for the period between 1689 and the end of the eighteenth century.[11] Population directed to the Volga regions constituted another significant flow: concerned to consolidate her eastern holdings, Catherine the Great pursued a true immigration policy that lasted till the end of the century. Other German migrants traveled to the Black Sea at the end of the century, while a significant group also moved into Poland.

Another important vector of conquest and settlement, especially in the eighteenth century, lay within the Russian Empire and pointed south and to the Black Sea. In addition to the Germanic colonies along the Volga, the colonization of Novorossiya got under way in 1764, a region that stretched from the Bug to the Seversky Donets Rivers and constituted at the time the imperial frontier. Following defeat of the Turks in the Russo–Turkish War of 1768–74 and definitive acquisition of the Crimea by Russia in 1783, that colonization was consolidated during Potemkin's governorship of the Novorossiya and Azov. As McNeill writes:

> By 1706, therefore, when the Empress Catharine II died, the Russian flood had engulfed the once-formidable Tartar society, reducing the remnant to a culturally decapitated, economically impoverished and politically helpless enclave. All the vast steppe region north of the Crimea and west of the Don had been occupied by landlords and settlers.[12]

It is estimated that between 1724 and 1859, the Russian population in the New South grew from 1.6 to 14.5 million, thanks to migrants coming from central and northern Russia to the black earth and steppes of the south. Nonetheless, this vast area was still sparsely populated at the end of the eighteenth century, with not more than 7–8 inhabitants per square kilometer.

Finally, the issue of border security with the Turkish Empire inspired Austria to encourage various groups – for the most part Germanic – to establish agricultural colonies along the frontier, especially along the Danube and from the Sava confluence to the Iron Gate. This was another case in which careful planning, abundant available land, good agricultural technology, and the introduction of new crops (potatoes and tobacco) helped make this migration a success. At the end of Maria Theresa's reign, immigration came more or less to a stop as all the land had been taken up by colonists who had in turn established a Germanic society along the southwest border of the empire.

Other international migrations were in reality processes of osmosis between contiguous regions, as, for example, that taking place between the end of the fifteenth century and the first third of the seventeenth century and directed from southern France to Aragon, Valencia, and especially Catalonia. It has been estimated that in the second half of the sixteenth century, one Catalan in five had been born outside Catalonia. Other examples include: Galicians going to Portugal; Albanians to the Adriatic coast of Italy; and Swiss, after the Thirty Years War, to Alsace, the Palatinate, and southern Germany. Further north, migrants moved from Germany, Flanders, and Norway to Holland; and from Scotland to Ireland and England. These population movements were inspired by strong economic differentials, helped by the absence of political and legal barriers, and served to fill gaps created by wars and other mortality crises. In addition to migrations of this sort, responding – we would say today – to market forces, there were others of a political nature, in particular those inspired by religious intolerance. The expulsion of Jews, and especially Moriscos, created serious gaps in the social and economic fabric of the Iberian Peninsula. They also had a demographic impact: the Jews expelled in 1492 exceeded 90,000 and the Moriscos – for the most part descendants of indigenous converts to Islam and so ethnically (but not culturally) homogeneous with the rest of the Spanish population – expelled in 1609–14 numbered between 300 and 350 thousand. The latter figure amounted to about 5 percent of the entire population: one inhabitant in eight in Murcia, one in five in Aragon, and one in four in Valencia.[13] Between 1530 and the beginning of the seventeenth century, large numbers of Anabaptists and Calvinists were expelled from the southern provinces of the Netherlands and moved to the northern ones, to the German states, and to England. Emigration of the Huguenots following revocation of the Edict of Nantes was numerically less significant: from 1685 to 1690, between 140 and 160 thousand emigrants left a French population that at the time was almost four times as large as that of Spain.[14] It is difficult to quantify the many migrations inspired by religion that criss-crossed the European continent in the modern era. While the demographic impact on both sending and receiving countries may have been slight, the economic and social impact was considerable. Contributions to the receiving countries in particular were important. Cities like Frankfurt and Hamburg benefitted from the arrival of Protestants booted out of the Netherlands. The Huguenots contributed to the development of tapestry, glass, paper, and agriculture in Brandenburg; silk, gold, and clock-making in England; and banking in Switzerland.[15] Finally, the migration of specialized workers began to play an important economic role as they began in Europe to constitute a global market with its own ethnic and geographic characteristics: engineers of canals, dams, and mines; physicians and scientists; military officers; artists and musicians; textile workers and ceramicists; bureaucrats and merchants.

Beginning in 1500, as already discussed, Europe became a significant exporter of human resources, and transoceanic migration played an important role in economic development. Atlantic Europe played the main role in this regard, with limited contributions from elsewhere. Technological improvements in navigation were the necessary precondition. Consider the first great transoceanic voyage: 2,500 passengers taken from Spain to Santo Domingo aboard 32 ships in 1502. Each ship carried on average 80 people between passengers and crew, in addition to provisions, water, and baggage; also on board were foodstuffs for the colony, tools, raw materials, seeds, plants, and live animals. It was the first true voyage to populate the island with Europeans: by the end of the decade Santo Domingo was said to hold 10,000 Spanish colonists, including a considerable number of women. The existence of a demographic colony relied on a regular traffic between the island and the metropole able to transport people, goods, and information back and forth. Already by the decade 1506–15, the number of ships leaving Spain for the New World averaged about 30 per year, transporting a couple of thousand passengers: not a huge number but sufficient to initiate demographic colonization. Between 1590 and 1620, that traffic peaked as about 100 ships per year crossed the Atlantic. Based on registers kept at the Casa de Contratación in Seville that recorded ships' passages and cargos – both increased over time – it has been estimated that between 1500 and 1650, 450,000 Spaniards crossed the Atlantic never to come back. Some believe this figure underestimates the scale of the phenomenon.[16]

Similar stories can be told regarding British migration to North America and the Caribbean, and Portuguese migration to Brazil. Net migration out of England (all destinations but mostly North America) has been estimated at 270,000 between 1541 and 1600, 713,000 in the seventeenth century, and 517,000 in the eighteenth century. Emigration from Portugal was still more intense in relation to its small size: estimates put annual emigration in the sixteenth and seventeenth centuries at 4,000, and 9,000 in the eighteenth century, following the discovery of precious metals in Brazil.[17] Portugal's logistic and organizational capabilities allowed it to sponsor the migration of 4,000 families from the Azores and Madeira, in 1747, equipped with the necessary supplies to colonize the island of Santa Catarina and the adjacent Brazilian mainland.[18] Of the great colonial empires, only France – the most populous nation in Europe – supplied a small number of emigrants: the migratory flow to Canada was modest and numbered only 27,000 between 1600 and 1730. Migration to the Antilles was also slight. Among the non-colonial states, migration was significant from the German lands, estimated at between 125 and 200 thousand over the course of the eighteenth century. Nor were the Americas the only destination. During nearly two centuries of operation (1602–1795), the Dutch East Indies Company (VOC) transported about a million Europeans to Asian and African ports; about half returned and about half stayed (many of the latter succumbing to a quick death).[19]

From a purely demographic point of view, emigration was modest. On the other hand, the migrants' level of reproductive fitness was high, as discussed in chapter 2, and by 1800 there were some 7 million inhabitants of European extraction in the Americas – descendants of that modest migratory stream. They had by then stamped a European imprint on an entire continent in terms of language, religion, cities, technology, and even (with some limitations) the physical environment. The elements needed to attract and accommodate the great migrations of the nineteenth century were all in place.

Summing up, although the European population in the period considered here was for the most part tied to the land, it was far from immobile; nor was European mobility only local or short-range. There arose instead centers of labor demand capable of periodically attracting the migration of hundreds of thousands of workers. For specialized workers, there developed a truly continental labor market. A process of urbanization was under way that attracted – and repelled – immigrants not only from the nearby rural hinterland, but also from farther afield. That migration served to compensate for the chronic urban demographic deficit and so fed the growth of cities. Ethnic and religious considerations inspired other migrations, and, finally, intercontinental migration developed, as several million Europeans, coming for the most part from the imperial powers, crossed the oceans. We can close with three observations. First, short-, medium-, and long-range migration was an important force in the history of early modern Europe and brought with it complex demographic, economic, and social ramifications. Migration was not a peripheral phenomenon, but instead a structural component of social life. Second, this intense mobility – the ability to move from place to place – derived from the strengthening of human capital, a process nourished also by technological innovations. And, third, at the end of the eighteenth century, the innovations brought about by the Industrial Revolution bore fruit in a society for which the physical change of residence was a normal occurrence. Europe was poised for the mass migration of the following century.

− 5 −

A Quickening Pace
1800–1913

During the long nineteenth century, the pace of migration and mobility quickened: the overall rate of change accelerated, differences widened, distances became shorter, and contact between different worlds became more intense. The facility of moving from one place to another, an essential component of human capital, increased, as did the number of people on the move, whether traveling near or far, temporarily or permanently, by choice or at times by force. The individual qualities that favored or constrained migration also changed and so that fitness that is at the heart of migratory selection processes. In Europe, the open and sparsely inhabited spaces that had previously attracted immigration and settlement had filled up. The "new worlds" outside of Europe that had received a steady trickle of migration over the previous three centuries had by now entered firmly into the European sphere of action – in spite of the dissolution of the American colonies – and were tied to Europe by institutional, cultural, religious, and linguistic affinities. Other worlds opened in Oceania and sub-Saharan Africa, regions that were rich in both land and natural resources but sparsely populated and so open to European expansion.

To better understand the long-distance migration of the nineteenth century and how it compares to that of the preceding centuries, it will be useful to first consider some of the demographic, social, and economic changes on which it depended. The first ingredient was rapid population growth, especially in the countryside. That growth combined with gradually increasing agricultural productivity to produce an ever larger segment of underpaid or unemployed rural labor. At the same time, the industrial sector grew and so attracted and offered employment to those excess rural workers. Finally, the acceleration of global economic integration created a system that sought to achieve equilibrium without attention to national borders. These phenomena are all connected and none by itself (or joined to just one of the others) could have precipitated the mass migrations of the nineteenth century. And massive they were: the "net export" of human resources between the beginning of the nineteenth century and the end of World War I amounted to about 50 million people (from a population that in 1800 numbered approximately 188 million), several dozen times greater than the net migration that took place during any of the three previous centuries. It was then a large and systemic phenomenon that had an impact on the entire continent, not simply a partial adjustment made by a rural society with strong ties to the land.

Natural growth caused the population of Europe to increase by a factor of 2.5 between 1800 and 1913 (eve of World War I); from 188 to 458 million inhabitants. Over the preceding three centuries, that population had barely doubled, and even that modest growth had created strains on resources in a context of limited land availability and stagnant or slowly increasing agricultural productivity. Over the course of the nineteenth century, those checks that had kept mortality high were relaxed: the availability of food resources became less precarious and indeterminate; medical knowledge improved and so did the defense against infectious diseases. Gradually, then, mortality declined, and with a few decades of lag time so did fertility. For a time, the separation between fertility and mortality curves (which is to say the rate of natural increase or the difference between birth rates and death rates) became a gaping one, producing the population increase described above. Then, in the second half of the nineteenth century, birth control gradually increased – a natural adaptation by families that would otherwise have had to support more children than they could manage as a result of the mortality decline – and so fertility declined. In the twentieth century, the gap between the two curves once again became small (though at much lower levels than before). This process has been called the "demographic transition" and caused the annual growth rate to reach as high as 1 percent – four or five times what it had been in the past – in spite of emigration. Growth was even more rapid in the countryside where birth control practices were adopted at a slower pace than they were in the cities.

Economic transformation constitutes the second contributing factor: the Industrial Revolution that was accompanied and preceded by a less obvious "Agricultural Revolution." Outside of England, where the Industrial Revolution was already in full swing, at the beginning of the nineteenth century about three-quarters of the European population worked in agriculture, resided in the countryside, and lived according to rules that had been well-established for centuries. The agricultural productivity of this population began to increase for a number of reasons: shortened fallow times, land reclamation, new crops, better tools, artificial selection of seed strains and livestock, and eventually the introduction of agricultural machinery. The approximate dating of the agricultural revolution places its start around 1700 (or earlier) in England; the second half of the eighteenth century in France, Switzerland, Germany, and Denmark; around 1820–30 in Austria, Sweden, and Italy; and around 1860–70 in Russia and Spain. According to Bairoch, labor productivity increased by about 0.6 percent per year between 1800 and 1850, 0.9 percent between 1850 and 1880, and 1.2 percent between 1880 and 1910.[1] This was an impressive increase and coincides with the increasing importance of emigration over the course of the century. The double pressure created by demographic growth and increased productivity brought with it complex consequences: negative pressure on real wages, fragmentation of property holdings and impoverishment of smallholders, and an increase in landless families. It was natural that the pressure to emigrate increased. But emigrate where? Except in Russia, there was no new land to farm. Grigg has calculated that cultivable land in Europe grew only slightly, from 140 to 147 million hectares, between 1860 and 1910.[2] In that same period, the land farmed in Canada, the United States, and Argentina grew by 100 million hectares. Moreover, low production costs in the Americas and a drop in transportation costs caused food prices to fall and plunged the European countryside into crisis, beginning in the 1870s. Nor did these pressures only generate migration across national borders and outside of Europe. Significant chunks of population were also absorbed by industrialization. Those same forces that had stimulated agricultural growth and increased productivity also fed the industrialization process. That development combined with the growth of cities, and so the service sector provided important outlets for redundant rural population. While three-quarters of the European labor force had been employed in agriculture in 1800, that figure declined to about half by 1850 and one third by the early twentieth century. Until 1850, the total size of the agricultural labor force had been growing, after which it stabilized and began to decline by the century's end. The continent became ever less rural as manufacturing, mining, and construction became more important, along with what we refer to today as the tertiary sector. Urbanization was intense: the population of the 39 European cities with populations over 100,000 in 1850 grew from 6 million in 1800 to 34 million in 1910, an almost sixfold increase.

Small and medium-sized cities experienced similar growth, multiplying the openings for work in administration, shipping, trade, and services.

Gradually, as European industry developed and so labor demand, the pressure to emigrate lessened. From the late nineteenth to the early twentieth centuries, emigration and industrialization bore an inverse relationship: when the number of workers employed in industry approached that in agriculture, transatlantic emigration dropped off. In Great Britain, during the last decades of the nineteenth century, industrial workers outnumbered agricultural ones and mass emigration was a thing of the past. Prior to World War I, workers in industry outnumbered those in agriculture in Belgium – which had never experienced mass emigration – and in Germany and Switzerland where emigration had ceased. By contrast, in Mediterranean countries like Italy and Spain, where industrialization really only took hold in the decades after World War II, emigration also dropped off in that period. In other countries (Holland, Sweden, Norway), where industrial work became important in the interwar period, emigration had halted earlier because of the economic crisis.

Restructuring in agriculture, then, often a cause of social disruption and impoverishment, fed emigration that was only partially absorbed by industrialization and urban growth. Meanwhile, the world embarked on a process of economic integration as Europe became ever more closely connected with the other continents. Migration responded effectively to economic cycles of expansion and contraction and to labor demand overseas. Europe possessed an excess of human resources and so began to export them in massive quantities across the ocean, and along routes already well traveled. The time needed to complete those voyages, moreover, had decreased, thanks to the introduction of steamships. At the beginning of the eighteenth century, the crossing aboard sailing ships was not much faster than it had been in Columbus's day: five or six weeks from Liverpool to New York. In 1838, the *Great Western* steamship crossed the Atlantic in 15 days, and by the 1880s the trip was normally completed in about a week. It took 38 days to get from Spain (Galicia) to Cuba under sail power in the 1850s; steamships made the trip in about 10 days by 1900. Costs dropped in tandem: a trip from England to the US, that cost 44 dollars in the 1850s, cost only 20 in the 1880s. In the 1870s, it still cost over 50 dollars to travel from Spain to South America; at the beginning of the twentieth century, that ticket only cost 35.[3] Expansion of the rail network, moreover, made it easier to reach the embarkation ports.

Political changes also gradually broke down barriers to European emigration and encouraged migration to the Americas. In its colonial era, Spain had placed numerous obstacles and restrictions on emigration to America. And, generally speaking, mercantilist policies were hostile to emigration, though rarely to the extent reached in Austria where emigration was for a time considered treasonous.[4] In England and the Scandinavian countries, emigration controls had already been lifted by the 1830s. Elsewhere, that development came later: in Germany, following reordering of the Confederation in 1867, and in Austria, Hungary, and Russia, toward the end of the century. A truly liberal emigration policy was only introduced in Italy in 1901; before that date, there still existed a host of controls. In the kingdom of Naples, "police did not permit travel even between provinces without a passport [...] and that passport, coming from Naples, could normally not be obtained in less than three months."[5] In Spain, heavy controls, bans, and other burdens were not relaxed until near the end of the century. Policies in the receiving countries instead encouraged immigration. The US Homestead Act of 1862 granted land at no cost to heads of families, aged at least 21, who planned to farm the land and either were, or had applied to become, US citizens. In 1873, Argentina introduced a policy that actively encouraged immigration, including the creation of special immigrant assistance and employment offices, financing of internal transfers, and free lodging for immigrants arriving in the port of Buenos Aires. Starting in 1888, Brazil financed transatlantic voyages and helped the immigrants acquire land in designated areas.[6]

Demographic growth, agricultural revolution, and globalization are the three fundamental forces that help to explain how European emigration over the course of the nineteenth century achieved the scale that it did. Which is not to say that other forces were not also at work: crisis following the Napoleonic era; the Irish famine of 1846–7 and those that followed in Scandinavia; pogroms carried out against the Jews in Russia; economic crisis in the 1890s; the abolition of slavery in Brazil and the ensuing crisis for coffee plantations deprived of low-cost labor. All of these events, however, only served to accelerate a process that derived primarily from a profound transformation of the traditional rural world.

Stanley Johnson described the effects of population pressure a century ago:

A case in point was offered by Rum in the Hebrides. The proprietor of this island found, in 1825, that his rents were £300 in arrears. A visit to the locality conclusively showed him that the indebtedness of the people was not due to any lack of industry on their part, but that the overcrowded numbers precluded any of them from gaining an adequate livelihood. Recognising that matters could never improve of themselves, he cancelled their debts, shared a sum of £600 amongst them, gave them cattle, and paid their passage out to Canada. Later on, it is recorded that this proprietor had repeopled his little island on a less crowded basis and was deriving £800 per annum as rent from it.[7]

This particular case, given the foresight of the proprietor and the setting in the far north of Europe, seems a Malthusian parable, but similar mechanisms were at work in many parts of the continent. Another commentator, writing at the same time as Johnson, identified disruption of the

traditional rural equilibrium as the driving force behind
the population exodus:

> The results of the breakup of the old system of land holding
> were often disastrous. The peasant being free to divide his
> land and feeling that his children all had equal claims, cut
> up land which was only sufficient to support one house-
> hold among a number of descendants. The landholder
> unable to support himself from his own plot sought to eke
> out his living by working for wages in a population where
> few could afford to hire labor. In some districts debts,
> contracted under circumstances which put the borrower at
> the mercy of a Jewish creditor, worked havoc.
>
> Thus the peasant with mortgage payments which he
> could not meet or with children for whom he could not
> provide an adequate patrimony, saw himself face to face
> with an intolerable decline of social status for himself and
> his children; namely, reduction to the position of property-
> less day laborer. This is the sting which induces many a
> man among the Slovaks, the Poles, the Ruthenians, to fare
> over seas or to send out his son to the new land from which
> men come back with savings.[8]

Beginning in the 1830s, European emigration took on
mass proportions. Citing only the major senders, estimates
for 1840 to 1932 put total departures for overseas destinations at 18 million for Great Britain and Ireland, 11.1
million for Italy, 6.5 million for Spain and Portugal, 5.2
million for Austria-Hungary, 4.9 million for Germany,
2.9 million for Poland and Russia, and 2.1 million for
Sweden and Norway. In terms of major destinations, this
mass of emigrants – who also created a significant wave of
return migration – went to the United States (34.2 million),
Argentina and Uruguay (7.1 million), Canada (5.2 million),
Brazil (4.4 million), Australia and New Zealand (3.5
million), and Cuba (0.9 million). Emigration peaked in the
first 15 years of the twentieth century when between 1 and
1.5 million Europeans per year migrated overseas, a current
equal to one third of the excess of births over deaths in

that same period. Subsequently, the Great War and then US immigration restrictions drastically reduced that current. In the last two decades of the nineteenth century, migration to North America – about triple that going to the rest of the continent – changed its make-up: a population of primarily British, German, and Scandinavian origin was infiltrated by Mediterraneans (above all Italians), Eastern Europeans, and Balkans. This was a "new" immigration, geographically and culturally more remote than the "old" one. That change in the composition of the US population, together with economic and social changes, lay behind the restrictive laws introduced in the 1920s.

The migrations of the long nineteenth century had a significant impact on both sending and receiving societies, not only because of the net transfer of population across the ocean, but also from longer-term transformations. Given that the migrants were on average young and characterized by high fertility, their contribution to demographic growth was still greater than their numbers might have predicted. For the United States, where population increased tenfold between 1800 and 1913, a simple estimate suggests that the immigrant contribution to demographic growth for the period 1840–1920 varied between one fifth and one third.[9] That figure was much higher in Argentina or Australia. These calculations are, however, simplifications of a complex phenomenon, and there are better methods of evaluation. International rural-to-rural migration, as most of it was in the early part of the nineteenth century, required stable families with large numbers of children. Families of that sort were poorly equipped for survival in the sending regions – in the clutches of a Malthusian trap created by population pressure and scarce resources – but well suited to the destination countries where land was abundant and so a large family of workers an advantage. Similarly advantageous were the traditional social and family values of those migrants. Migration from the countryside to cities and industrial regions, where workers were employed primarily as wage laborers in manufacturing and construction, favored instead a different profile, namely, workers who were mobile and with few ties: individuals whose family ties were looser as the family members had stayed behind; nuclear families able to carefully plan births; and individuals equipped to exploit innovations and knowledge to improve their social standing. The rapid adjustment of immigrant fertility to that of receiving regions (see chapter 2) can be interpreted as an adaptive strategy. We might cite as a general example of successful migration the arrival of Jews from the Eastern European Pale of Settlement in the US, the adaptation and social rise of whom has been so masterfully described by Philip Roth.[10]

Historically, migration has been a tool for improving one's standard of living (a general concept that goes well beyond simple economic considerations). Nomadic populations in search of ecosystems richer in resources were seeking to improve their standard of living, as were those first farmers who constituted the prehistoric waves of human expansion, medieval and early modern migrants, and also those transoceanic migrants of the nineteenth and twentieth centuries. One might also migrate to escape the worsening of one's standard of living caused by political or religious persecution, environmental degradation, or war. In any case, except for forced migration, the choice to migrate always involves a complex balancing of costs and benefits carried out by individuals, families, and communities. Nor can that balancing be reduced to a simple economic calculation, but entails instead a mixture of certain and less certain assessments, thoughts about the present and the future, material considerations and more idealistic ones. Just the same, there is no denying that differences in material conditions between sending and receiving countries has played a major role in the modern history of migration. John Kenneth Galbraith has in fact written that it was migration that broke the historic equilibrium of poverty that characterized the European countryside. That equilibrium was based on a forced accommodation to seemingly immutable poverty. It was an entirely rational form of adaptation to a situation in which the irrational response was instead to fight constantly and futilely against that poverty. Emigration allowed a way out:

> For most of those who have attempted it, it has served well. For their children even better. It has only rarely required any active effort on the part of governments. More often it has needed only their acquiescence and, most often, in recent times, only their nonvigilance. It has placed no strain on the capacity for public action of the poor countries. Where fully exploited, it has not only involved the escape from poverty for those directly involved, but it has facilitated escape within the equilibrium of poverty for those motivated to a different course [...] As a remedy for poverty, it focuses with precision on those for whom such a policy is alone workable and for whom it must be designed – those who, rejecting accommodation, are motivated to improve their economic position. No effort or money is wasted on those who are not yet so motivated.[11]

Successful migration, then, selects those with a solid motivation, individuals who reject this "accommodation" and are able to exploit the opportunities offered by economic disparities between sending and receiving countries.

European experience in the long nineteenth century also helps us to correct a contemporary commonplace, namely, the idea that in poor countries it is the absence of development that is the cause of emigration and so by supporting development population pressure will diminish. That analysis misinterprets the development process that instead almost always disrupts or destroys rural society and so in the short and medium term increases rather than reduces migration pressure:

> In peasant economies, output is determined not by markets but by the size and composition of households, and economic and social relations are predicated on assumptions

of stability and continuity. Economic development necessarily destroys this stable social and economic system
through three mutually reinforcing processes: the substitu-
tion of capital for labor, the privatization and consolidation of landholding, and the creation of markets. The
destruction of the peasant political economy creates a pool
of socially and economically displaced people with weakened ties to the land, the community, and the past ways of
life. These displaced rural dwellers provide the source for
both internal and international migrants.[12]

This point is worth recalling both in relation to the past
and the future. The first phase of development in the
poorest African countries is causing disruption of the sort
that once afflicted rural Europe, creating conditions that
favor emigration.

− 6 −

The Last Century
The Trend Reverses, 1914–2010

An animated depiction of migration flows over the past century between Europe and the rest of the world would suggest a schizophrenic continent where the trends break off suddenly, reverse direction, and make wild leaps. It has been a century during which the ability to move from place to place – much facilitated by changes in technology and infrastructure, economic development, and the expansion of markets – has been constantly hindered, blocked, and regulated by political considerations, both internal and external. The major events in this regard have included: two world wars and the geopolitical changes they occasioned, including border changes and forced population movements; the crisis of 1929 and the isolationism that followed, reversing a process of economic and migratory internationalization that had begun in 1870; the division of Europe with the consolidation of the Soviet Bloc and the interruption of movement between East and West, and then the break-up of that division; the birth, consolidation, and expansion of the European Union and the creation of a large area of free circulation among states (even if more in theory than in practice); and finally decolonization and the shift for the great powers from being sources of international emigration to destinations for international immigration.

In addition to these events and processes – which would take a great deal of space to describe – there is an underlying force that has played a fundamental role over the past century. Since the beginning of the twentieth century, the demographic transition has entered into its mature phase: fertility dropped dramatically, reaching historic lows at the end of the century, and so population growth has slowed. Europe has ceased to produce those excess human resources that fed the great migrations of the nineteenth century; mortality has come to exceed fertility in ever larger parts of the continent, and population momentum has flagged. And yet the population of Europe grew from 488 million in 1914 to 733 million in 2010. Between 1914 and 1950, 60 million were added (+12 percent) in spite of the human losses inflicted by war, catastrophe, and epidemic.[1] There is no precise measurement of the toll taken by disasters, but direct military losses in 1914–18 were about 9 million in the belligerent states to which have to be added losses in the Russian civil war of 1918–21 (apparently several million).[2] Losses in World War II were higher still given the involvement of civilian populations, persecutions and massacres, and the near extermination of the Jews; the extent of the tragedy is estimated at between 38 and 52 million deaths. The Spanish flu epidemic may have cost another 2 million lives. Losses due to famine in the Volga regions in 1921 are not well measured, but numbered in the millions; while that which devastated the Ukraine, Caucasus, and other parts of the Soviet Union in 1932–3 (the product of political decisions) cost between 9 and 12 million lives.[3] Although approximate, these figures give some idea of the huge demographic price paid for the madness of the twentieth century; and to all those victims should be added net emigration that amounted to about 6 million departures in the 1920s. In spite of all these losses, the European population continued to grow, if at a slower pace. It would continue to grow in the post-war decades, thanks to a brief fertility recovery supported by positive economic trends: between 1950 and 1970 population increased by 109 million (+20 percent). After 1970, growth slowed and population increase dropped to 65 million (+10 percent) in 1970–90, and just 18 million (+2.5 percent) in 1990–2010. Over the past 20 years, had it not been for immigration from outside of Europe, the population would have shrunk, rather than increased, because of the very low fertility of the genera-tions born after the last war.

In the second half of the twentieth century, that long cycle of growth that had begun several centuries before, with the joint action of the Industrial Revolution and the demographic transition, came to an end. That cycle produced a fivefold increase in population and real per-sonal incomes that grew by a factor of 20.[4] It was a cycle during which Europe grew economically, thanks to its abundant demographic resources, and it is now certainly concluded. The third millennium marks instead the beginning of a new cycle characterized by limited or decreasing demographic resources (if not supplemented by immigration); nor can we gauge how long it will last. Moreover, while Europe's demographic vitality fed con-tinued steady emigration in much of the twentieth century, it proceeded at a slower pace than previously: the net migratory deficit for 1920–40 amounted to 7 million, and for 1950–70 about 4 million. The inversion of the cycle instead took place in the last third of the century, as Europe experienced a net migratory gain of 8 million in 1970–90 and another 27 million during 1990–2010. That shift, as already noted, marked the end of 500 years of migration history after which the conti-nent that had contributed to populating the Americas, Oceania, southern Africa, and Siberia became instead an importer of human resources. Within the complex context of the twentieth century, we need to explore these fun-damental changes a bit further in order to better under-stand their causes and consequences.

As the twentieth century moved into its final phase, the conditions that had made the great transoceanic migration possible ceased to be. Labor demand slackened in the traditional receiving countries as labor supply in Europe also declined in tandem with slower demographic growth. While these phenomena acted gradually, other factors interrupted migratory flows more abruptly, namely, wars and state policies. Europe's net loss to emigration during the decade 1905–14 was 14 million. Following the interruption of the war, that figure dropped to 6 million between 1921 and 1930, and then again to little more than a million between 1930 and 1940. The most effective brakes on migration were the restrictions adopted in the United States, culminating in the National Origin Act of 1924 that not only established an annual ceiling for immigration (a little over 150,000, about a sixth of the pre-war level), but also penalized especially the areas of "new immigration," namely Southern and Eastern Europe. The quota for Italy, which had supplied about a quarter of the pre-war immigration, was reduced to less than 4 percent of total admissions. As a result of the Great Depression, other receiving countries imposed their own restrictions and quotas: South Africa in 1930, New Zealand in 1931, Australia in 1932, and Brazil in 1934. For a variety of reasons – pressure to exclude ethnic, cultural, or religious groups; economic difficulties; or the conviction that societies created by immigration had attained stable dimensions – the great era of European migration was over. The brief revival after World War II took place in a different context, and finds its explanation in family reunification and the settlement of refugees more than in labor migration. This is not to say that the migratory links between Europe and the other continents were broken in the second half of the century, but they were of lesser importance and without great demographic impact, marginal in terms of development except for the cases of Canada and Australia. The convergence of standards of living between Europe and the Americas lessened the pressure to migrate; Europe's demographic decline began to generate its own immigration; and the vast reservoir of labor south of the Rio Grande offered labor at a good price for the wealthy part of North America.

In spite of developments in transportation, more intense communication, and the growth of cultural links and knowledge, the second half of the twentieth century saw Europe become more distant from those parts of the world that it had helped to populate. The human, family, and economic ties that tens of millions of Europeans had established with societies overseas weakened and disappeared. Italy, for example, was more "cosmopolitan" a century ago than it is today. The earlier cosmopolitanism came from below, from the proletariat, and was based on real-life experience. Today's cosmopolitanism (if we can call it that) is based on the media, on fleeting contacts, and sporadic visits. America in the second half of the twentieth century was paradoxically farther from Europe than it had been at the beginning of the century.

In addition to the losses we have already described, the two world wars forced migratory shifts within the European continent. Although this book has focused primarily on spontaneous or voluntary migration, the post-war transfers merit mention for a couple of reasons. The first is that the forces unleashed by the twentieth-century wars brought about upheavals rarely matched in history, and central to those catastrophes was migration. The second is that those forced transfers were often the origin of return migrations in subsequent decades.

The outbreak of war in 1914 created a flow of return migration because of military conscription, the disruption of trade and transportation, and expulsions from belligerent countries. As Dudley Kirk has written:

> The peace, rather than the war, caused the greatest permanent displacement of population. Changes in international boundaries resulted in large movements from the ceded territories, composed of government officials, persons dispossessed of their property, and others who had little

future under the new regimes. These were supplemented by forced population exchanges in Eastern Europe with the objective of securing greater ethnic unity in the new states.[5]

The transfers affected Germany, with the ceding of Alsace-Lorraine to France and other territories to Poland; the states that emerged from the break-up of Austria-Hungary; and above all the exchanges between Greece and Turkey following the Lausanne Treaty of 1922. In all, these international transfers have been estimated to involve 5 million people.

The territorial changes after World War II were more limited in extent, though the associated population transfers were much greater. The Eastern territories of the German Reich saw the division of Eastern Prussia between the Soviet Union and Poland and the ceding of Pomerania and Silesia, also to Poland. In addition, those Polish territories with Belarusian and Ukrainian majorities were transferred to the USSR. In all, 11–12 million Germans were moved out of the Balkans, the Sudetenland, and the territories ceded to the USSR and Poland, a sort of *Drang nach Osten* in reverse, seven or eight centuries after the original.[6] Nor should we overlook the fact that the Nazi war effort required the forced labor of millions of foreigners (7.5 million in 1944, of whom 1.8 million were prisoners of war).[7] Other territorial adjustments – Finnish, Czech, and Romanian lands to the USSR; Italian territory to Yugoslavia – had limited demographic impact.

The three decades between 1914 and 1945 can be interpreted as a sort of parenthesis interrupting the long-term forces that dominated the nineteenth and twentieth centuries. We can imagine that without that parenthesis, the great transoceanic migration would have declined more gradually and internal migration in Europe would have developed as a function of the structural changes, agricultural and industrial, initiated in the nineteenth century. In the 50 years preceding World War I, the growth of industry and emerging globalization reinforced migration within

Europe, especially that directed to France, Switzerland, Belgium, and Germany. Four out of 10 Italian emigrants in the period 1890–1915 went to European destinations. Between the wars, this mechanism slowed dramatically for two reasons, one of which followed upon the other. The first was the decimation of the younger generations in war. The second was the economic Depression and unemployment, protectionist economic policies, and strict migration controls, especially in the dictatorships. Nonetheless, migration within Europe did not come to a complete halt after the war and indeed revived some. In the 1920s, migration into France – which had suffered dramatic losses in the war: 1.4 million deaths and 1.5 million disabled – picked up, resulting in a net increase of about 2 million people, mostly Poles and Italians. Infrastructure needed rebuilding, and gaps in the labor force needed to be filled, for coalmining, manufacturing, and agriculture. Immigration, which had been unfettered in the pre-war era, was at this point only partially free as many immigrants were recruited by agencies created by employers and the government.[8] In the 1930s, instead, with the onset of economic crisis and union pressure to protect French workers, a quota system with more strict rules was introduced, and the inflow came practically to a halt. Less significant currents flowed into Belgium, Holland, and Switzerland. In the 1930s and until the outbreak of the war, state controls on immigration tightened almost everywhere, while other currents responded to political forces: the repatriation of Turks leaving the Balkans, Jews going to Palestine, Italians to Africa, and refugees fleeing from the Spanish Civil War into France. Nazi rearmament absorbed hundreds of thousands of German workers coming from the Sudetes and Austria, both before and after annexation to the Reich.

In the interwar period, the European dualism between a rich and industrial Northwest and a poorer, rural South and East reflected a demographic dualism whereby growth was slowing down in the Northwest but still robust in the rest of the subcontinent. In spite of conflict and economic crisis, the economically strong and demographically weak regions continued to attract labor migration. In the quarter-century that followed World War II, a period characterized by the exclusion of all Eastern Europe from the market economy and strong economic development in the West, these structural transfers intensified. In the brief period between 1950 (when pre-war levels were re-achieved) and 1973 (year of the oil crisis), per capita income in Western Europe increased by a factor of 2.5. An abundant and flexible supply of labor aided reconstruction and growth, keeping both the cost of labor and prices low. In the economically stronger countries (Great Britain, France, Germany, Benelux), immigration contributed to the self-financing of businesses, international competitiveness, and geographic and sector mobility. In the weaker ones (Italy, Spain, Portugal, Greece), emigration lowered unemployment, while migrants' remittances contributed to improving the standard of living and certainly also to development. This same process was at work in markedly "dual" countries like Italy and Spain, where strong currents of internal migration flowed from south to north. According to the United Nations, between 1950 and 1970, Western Europe (France, Germany, Benelux, and Switzerland) absorbed a net immigration of 6.6 million, while Southern Europe (Italy, Spain, Portugal, Greece, Yugoslavia) generated a net emigration of about the same size (6.3 million). Immigration into the stronger countries, however, did not come exclusively from Southern Europe: Turks migrated to Germany, and population from the various former colonies (in the Indian subcontinent, the Caribbean, Indonesia, Indochina, and the Maghreb) flowed into the respective metropoles. Recruitment programs organized by employers, and carefully controlled by governments, accounted for much of this migration. In many cases, this immigration was treated as temporary, reflecting the official misconception that a society might take advantage of immigrant labor without taking on the burden of integration. We shall discuss these frustrated expectations below. The oil crisis of 1973–4 ended this migratory phase and led to a period of economic restructuring during which manufacturing shed workers, greater factor productivity became an important goal, and capital-intensive activities came to take the place of labor-intensive ones. Recruitment programs ceased, and immigration controls were tightened. Meanwhile, Southern Europe, till then a supplier of labor, experienced slowing population growth and the economic disparities within Europe lessened: in 1950, per capita income in France was 50 percent greater than that of Italy; in 1973, the difference had declined to 23 percent. In the 1970s, the Mediterranean countries ceased to be emigration countries and began instead to attract their own immigration.

The historic movement between the weaker and stronger parts of Europe, however, did not end in the 1970s. It had an epilogue in the 1990s, following the collapse of the Soviet Bloc and the entrance of the Warsaw Pact countries into the Western orbit. There ensued an East–West movement from Poland, Moldova, Romania, the broken-up bits of Yugoslavia, and the Balkans. With the expansion of the European Union, this migration has become more internal than international; nor can it last long as very low fertility is reducing the size of the younger generations in the countries from which this migration might come. Meanwhile, the great westward migration predicted to follow on the collapse and break-up of the Soviet Union never transpired, contrary to models based on the disparity of salaries and incomes. As it turned out, those repatriating to Russia from the former Soviet Republics far outnumbered the departures.

The historic transition, the moment when Europe went from being an exporter of human resources to an importer, took place in the 1970s. It has been estimated that between 1990 and 2010, Europe attracted a net immigration (so subtracting returnees) of 28 million: 4 million each were added to the North and East, 11 million to the South, and 9 million to the West.[9] Moreover, immigration coming from other continents – or in any case from outside the European Union (which has come to include about 90 percent of the European population outside the Russian Federation) – has, for the first time since the late Middle Ages, served not just an economic function but also a demographic one. Over the first decade of the present century, the indigenous population of young people has declined in Southern Europe, in Germany, and elsewhere. Immigration, then, has served to fill that gap, not to further European growth but to prevent economic retreat. At the heart of the phenomenon lies a demand for labor in activities that require limited skills, are poorly paid, and hold little interest for native labor. Even in a context of high unemployment, uncertainty, and low salaries, Europeans, protected by a social or familial safety net, avoid less desirable jobs; these are individuals accustomed to living in a prosperous society and enjoying high levels of consumption. To paraphrase Galbraith, they have accommodated the equilibrium of prosperity, just as the rural workers of past centuries accommodated the equilibrium of poverty. Finally, globalization has progressively expanded the areas from which immigrants arrive, from nearby north Africa to sub-Saharan Africa, to South America and Asia; though we should keep in mind that the current globalization is only a partial one, more a globalization of goods and trade than of human resources. In the nineteenth century, those human resources flowed with little obstruction from country to country, while today they are restricted by quotas and other strict selection mechanisms.

As of 2010, the European Union includes about 25 million immigrants who have arrived over the last few decades from outside of Europe, approximately 5 percent of the population.[10] That state of affairs – in the midst of the most serious economic crisis since the end of World War II – is the product of a complex process, strongly marked by political choices that have, nonetheless, failed to cancel out the underlying forces at work. That process can be synthesized as follows:

1   Europe's historic cycle of population growth has come to an end, and many European regions face potential demographic decline.
2   The migratory potential of the continent has declined, for demographic and economic reasons, and so the great transoceanic migration has also come to an end.
3   For a time, differential paths of development created marked economic and demographic disparities within Europe that followed similar geographic patterns and generated notable migration flows within Europe: East to West (between the wars and directed to France and the other Western powers), South to North (between World War II and the 1970s), and East to South and East to West (following the break-up of the socialist economies and continuing to the present day).
4   Immigration from poorer countries has taken off since the 1980s, owing largely to demand for unskilled labor and facilitated by the globalization process.
5   These population currents, however, have been impacted by restrictive policies, forced migrations, political discontinuities, and wars.
6   Finally, the demographic impact of immigration has been significant. Consider one example: according to UN estimates made a bit over a decade ago (1998), Spain and Italy were on the verge of demographic decline and ought to number 95 million inhabitants in 2010. In spite of correct methodology and excellent statistical data, that estimate was wide of the mark: the population of the two countries today is about 108 million, thanks to the contribution of immigrants and their offspring.[11]

Over the past two centuries, migratory processes have gradually sped up, losing that slow rhythm that characterized the waves of progress in earlier eras. At the same time, they have also intensified in quantitative terms. In 1570, following about 80 years of migration, Spaniards in the New World were less than 100,000. Romanians in Italy today number about 1 million, 10 times the Spanish figure and from an immigration that has lasted a tenth as long. We can roughly say that their potential impact on the host society (number times speed) is 100 times greater than that of the Spaniards in America. Obviously, this comparison leaves out considerations regarding military/political and technological differences, considerations which would enter into a more sophisticated model and would indeed reverse the above result.[12] It is not off the mark, however, to note that processes of interaction and integration between different groups are more effective when they occur gradually over time, and yet that gradualness is exactly what the present situation lacks. Finally, we might consider the factors contributing to the fitness of the migrants, a concept introduced in the opening chapters. That fitness is greater the more flexible, adaptable, and mobile the migrant. Family models play a role too: low fertility and a late age at marriage are advantages for migrants in the rich countries, just as is the ability to adapt (rather than abandon) traditional rules and values. These values are just the opposite of those that favored agricultural migrants in earlier eras, who drew their strength from solid and large families that conformed to traditional social norms.

– 7 –

Three Globalizations, Migration, and the Rise of America

Migration has served as a tool and a strategy of globalization in the modern era. In the mid-sixteenth century, the Americas risked depopulation following the shock of contact with Europe. And yet that did not come to pass, as a number of factors prevented the disaster: demographic recovery on the part of the indigenous populations, a continuous and at times intense flow of immigration, frequent cases of the mixings of peoples, and the "foundation effect" of certain groups. By about 1800, the entire continent had regained the level of population lost in the catastrophe, and the 25 million or so inhabitants at that time represented a number comparable, in terms of order of magnitude, to the population at the time of contact three centuries before. It was over the next two centuries, instead, that the Americas experienced irrepressible growth: between 1800 and 2000, the population doubled every 40 years – five times in all – and, as a percentage of the total population of the world, grew from 2.7 to 14 percent. Midway through the last century, their global economic weight reached as high as 40 percent of the total. The attraction exercised by the continent proved irresistible, and, for size and speed, growth exceeded all other parts of the world in recorded history. Moreover, it was America north of the Rio Grande that grew the fastest: accounting for little more than 20 percent of the continental population in 1800, that figure grew to 40 percent by 2000; and, over that same period, its share of the total continental economy grew from a quarter to two thirds.[1]

By the beginning of the twenty-first century, the ethnic and cultural make-up of the continent had been profoundly transformed, following a half millennium of migration. The indigenous population had progressively declined until it represented only a small minority. Europeans instead became the majority around the mid-eighteenth century, while Africans became established in spite of the many hardships that population endured. And Asians became a significant presence toward the end of the millennium. Data on the ethnic origins of the US population in 2000 reveal the outcome of centuries of continental interconnections: while a majority claims European ancestry, 31 million describe themselves as Latinos, 27 million as African Americans, 12 million as Asians, and 8 million as American Indian. In the second-largest American country, Brazil, the ethnic make-up is similarly complex, with a larger percentage of Africans and relatively greater ethnic mixing.[2]

The turbulent demographic and migratory history of the Americas is intimately bound up with a process of globalization that has gone through different phases and cycles. In order to clarify our discussion, it may be useful to consider three of these: a first phase – early colonialism – during which the Americas became firmly connected with the rest of the world; a second phase – from the mid-eighteenth century to World War I – that coincided with the spread of the Industrial Revolution; and a third phase that began with the end of World War II and continues to the present day. A restricted concept of globalization defines it as the integration of markets and the lowering of barriers to the free movement of goods, capital, and labor. The eighteenth-century integration of

markets, primarily Atlantic markets, translated in classic
fashion into a convergence of standards of living on both
sides of the ocean. O'Rourke and Williamson have given
a classic description of this phase of globalization:

> By 1914, there was hardly a village or town anywhere on
> the globe whose prices were not influenced by distant
> foreign markets, whose infrastructure was not financed by
> foreign capital, whose engineering, manufacturing, and
> even business skills were not imported from abroad, or
> whose labor markets were not influenced by the absence
> of those who had emigrated or by the presence of strangers
> who had immigrated. The economic connections were inti-
> mate, poor regions had enjoyed significant convergence
> gains by erasing part of the gap between themselves and
> rich regions, and flourishing exports sectors enjoyed the
> benefits associated with the global trade boom.[3]

In its broadest sense, "globalization" is not simply a
process of economic interconnection – of trade, finance,
and labor – but also a process of scientific, cultural, social,
political, and religious exchange. It is a polyvalent and dynamic interconnection that goes through phases of acceleration, slowing down, and stagnation. During moments
of growth, the opportunities for exchange between the
different parts of the world increase – including opportunities for the exchange of population – and the trans-
mission of forces between those parts also increases. In
this regard, America was a gigantic "island" until the establishment there of Europeans, Europeans who in a few
decades forged multiple and long-term links between
America and Europe, and America and Africa. According
to the royal cosmographer López de Velasco, by about
1570 there were 140,000 Spaniards settled in the continent, and another 20–30,000 Portuguese along the Atlantic coast of Brazil. Before the middle of that century, the
entire American continent had been explored: in 1541,

Valdivia founded Santiago in Chile; the next year, Orellana sailed down the Amazon from the Andes all the way to the ocean; and, in 1543, Coronado ventured as far as the Grand Canyon in the heart of what is today the United States. Every year dozens of ships crossed the Atlantic between Seville, Santo Domingo, and Portobelo, carrying people, animals, plants, seeds, tools, manufactures, gold, and silver (see chapter 4, pp. 43–4). Meanwhile an intense traffic of slave ships from Africa carried millions of captives over the following centuries. There developed in inter-connected segments what has quaintly been called "triangular trade:"

> In general, items manufactured in Europe, such as textiles, guns, and rum, were exchanged in Africa primarily for slaves. Slave ships then crossed the Atlantic in the infamous middle passage to American ports at which point the slaves who survived the ordeal were sold for cash, sugar, molasses, and other American products, depending on the location. Circuits also sailed from the Atlantic seaboard to the Caribbean to Europe and from New England to Africa to the Caribbean.[4]

Intercontinental links were also established across the much broader Pacific Ocean, seen by European eyes – those of Balboa and a group of his companions – for the first time in 1513. Manila was founded in 1517, and by the end of the century:

> the outlines of the East Indies and the China coast were tolerably clear, there was active trade with Japan, and a regular shipping line across the Ocean between Manila and Acapulco; the eastern shores from California to Tierra del Fuego were known to Europeans, and from Acapulco to Valdivia were the scene of a lively coastwise traffic. The northern coast of New Guinea was known, though Australia was scarcely imagined, unless as a hypothetic Terra Australis.[5]

Nearly a third of American silver (the vast majority of world production at the time) went to China, in exchange for luxury goods destined for European and American markets. In addition to silver, carmine, cacao, and other products traveled westward, while the return trade brought more varied merchandise. "Once a year the galleons from Manila would supply Acapulco with shipments including bundles of silk, cotton textiles, porcelains, cinnamon from Sri Lanka, and pepper from the Malabar coast. Sometimes slaves from southern Africa or lace from Flanders made the freight truly global."[6]

In the American case, this process of globalization was imposed by violence, by means of brutal conquest, domination, and subjugation of the entire continent, and the destruction of its religious, cultural, and political life; imposed in their places were European religion, language, and institutions. It was a process that bore little resemblance to those that followed in the nineteenth and twentieth centuries. Nor is it particularly useful to make that comparison, were it not for the fact that all depended on complex and relevant migrations. Immigrants followed the newly opened intercontinental pathways: it was migration fraught with difficulty, danger, and violence. The flow from Europe was modest, but often accompanied by a strong foundation effect. The flow of African slaves was more numerous, though the demographic impact was less given the harsh conditions under which they and their descendants toiled. European demand for New World products – precious metals and luxury woods, sugar and tobacco, skins and furs – brought about both the free and forced movement of peoples.

We can identify several different types of migration set in motion by this first phase of globalization. The first relates to the demand in the conquered territories for political, administrative, and religious personnel. We might call this "tertiary" migration, more political than economic, and consisting of the functionaries, administrators, religious, jurors, and soldiers needed to run the vast colonial domains. Though small in number, these migrants played a large role in determining the nature and evolution of colonial society, especially in the Iberian colonies. Another flow was expressly economic and consisted of a vigorous merchant class, technicians trained in mining and the working of metals, naval engineers, builders of infrastructure, artisans, and also farmers drawn by the abundant land made available. The Iberian societies in America were largely urban and recreated the fashions and lifestyles of the metropole, especially in large cities like Lima or Mexico City. Those experiments required the work of immigrants possessing specialized skills that could not be found among the indigenous labor force. In North America, and especially in New England and the Middle Colonies, the easy availability of land, and an institutional framework that protected private property, drew a significant flow of farmers.

A third flow was that of African slaves. It grew to massive proportions in response to the rapidly increasing demand created by the sugar plantations – especially in the Caribbean and Brazil – and the growing of tobacco and other colonial products for which there was a growing market in Europe. These activities required massive inputs of labor that could not be supplied by populations that were either in decline or on the way to extinction (in the Caribbean), or generally "ill-suited" or unavailable (the Indios in Brazil). The back-breaking labor required on the sugar plantations, as well as their harsh and at times brutal administration, has been well documented: the plowing, planting, and cutting of the cane; transportation to the sugar mills and distillation; and the cutting and transport of firewood over long distances to fuel the burners. These activities continued throughout the year, including nine months of production that required the constant operation of burners and mills and employed both men and women from dawn till dusk and, in the most intense periods, also at night.[7] The flow of slaves, which only peaked in the eighteenth century, amounted in the sixteenth and seventeenth centuries to about 1.5 million people. Of these, over 40 percent went to Brazil, a third to the Caribbean Islands, and the rest to mainland Spanish colonies, and, to a small degree, the English ones.

Migration from the British Isles to the North American colonies during the seventeenth century was small in number but highly significant in the long run: about 130,000 went to the Chesapeake (Virginia and Maryland), 24,000 to the Middle Colonies, and 21,000 to New England.[8] The largest flow went to Virginia and Maryland, in connection with the development of tobacco plantations to supply growing European demand. Tobacco cultivation was labor-intensive, and the Indians, small in number and poorly adapted to the work, were unable to satisfy the demand. Growers instead resorted to a particular sort of migration, namely, that of indentured servants who sold their labor to middle-men (often ships' captains), who in turn resold it to the landowners on arrival. Servitude might last four or five years; in reality, it was a form of fixed-term slavery. At the end of the contract, it was not unusual for the freed servant to receive a piece of land. Indentured servants from the British Isles (over 200,000 in the seventeenth century) also provided the initial labor force for plantations in the British Caribbean colonies, though they were rapidly replaced with African slaves in the second half of the century.[9] Here was a clear connection between globalization and migration: on one side of the Atlantic, an increase in the impoverished population and also in demand for colonial products; the establishment of stable communication between the two sides; and the development of plantations and strong labor demand, on the other side.

The establishment of stable intercontinental communication generated what we refer to today as "circular migration" (implying the return of emigrants to the sending country); though the numbers were small, that flow served to solidify the transoceanic link.

From the second half of the nineteenth century till the second decade of the twentieth, the process of economic integration between countries intensified and expanded geographically. Exports increased everywhere and at a greater rate than production. In the words of Angus Maddison, the period 1870–1913:

> was an era of improved communications and substantial factor mobility. There was a massive flow of foreign capital, particularly from the UK which directed about half its savings abroad. French and German investment were also very substantial, and there were significant flows from the USA and other countries ... British foreign assets were equivalent to about one and a half times its GDP, French assets about fifteen per cent more than GDP, German assets about 40 per cent, and US assets 10 per cent.[10]

Much investment went into railroads that expanded five-fold in North America between 1870 and 1913 (from 90,000 to 450,000 km), an undertaking that required masses of immigrant labor. In Latin America, the few thousand kilometers of rail in 1870 grew to 100,000 by 1913.[11] The growing economic integration between countries is well synthesized by the relationship between the value of exports and the domestic product of each country: in the United Kingdom, that figure grew from 3 percent in 1820 to 12 percent in 1870, to 18 percent in 1913; in France, for those same dates, the figures are 1, 5, and 8 percent; in Germany, they grew from 9 percent in 1870 to 16 percent in 1913.

Nineteenth-century economic integration had a profound impact on migration. We have already discussed (in chapter 5) the changes in Europe that made large segments of mostly rural population available for migration: increased demographic growth, increased productivity in agriculture, and so the creation of larger and larger groups of rural un- and under-unemployed, great improvements in transportation and the lowering of costs, and the easing of migration restrictions. On the demand side instead, need for labor grew in the Americas, rich in land but lacking in those workers that were instead abundant in small, densely populated Europe. Migration was then an integral part of the globalization process and led, among other things, to a degree of convergence between real wages in Europe and America, and between relative prices of other factors of production and rent for land that was abundant and cheap in America, but rare and expensive in Europe.[12] It was a convergence, however, that did not lead to a general leveling of economic development, as North America was simply growing faster. Between 1870 and 1913, per capita GDP in America grew at an annual rate of 1.8 percent as compared to 1.3 percent in Europe.[13]

At the end of the eighteenth century, the socio-ethnic make-up of North America (where the indigenous population was a small percentage) broke down to about four fifths European and one fifth African. In 1790, the first US census counted a black population of 757,000, 19.3 percent of the total. The great European migration of the nineteenth century significantly reduced the black percentage, bringing it down to 10.7 by 1920. The white population in 1790 was more than four fifths British (from Great Britain and Ireland), while the remaining fifth was mostly German (8.3 percent, mostly from the Palatinate), Franco-Belgian (3.4 percent), and Dutch (3.3 percent).[14]

The 34 million immigrants who arrived in the century after 1820 altered the earlier configuration, one that was strongly Northern European, and made it instead pan-European. Emigration from Europe came in partially overlapping waves that found their origins along a North–East–South trajectory (British, German, Scandinavian, Russian-Polish-Balkan, Mediterranean), a trajectory consistent with the spread of industrialization and Old World economic development.

The census of 1930 counted 39 million "foreign born" and "foreign or mixed parentage" (a third of the white population). Among that group, the British and Germans predominated (about 20 percent each), followed by Italians (10.9 percent), Scandinavians (9.2 percent), Poles (8.2 percent), Russians (6.8 percent), and then other Balkan and Mediterranean groups. But there were also significant groups of Chinese (almost 300,000 immigrants between the Gold Rush and 1882, after which their entry was severely limited) and Japanese (about half a million immigrants between 1885 and 1924, including Hawaii).[15]

The history of this stream of immigration is varied and complex, and it has been carefully described, analyzed, and interpreted. So we can limit ourselves to a few considerations related to globalization. More interesting to us than a description of the origin of these immigrants is their insertion into the American labor market, tied more to domestic economic growth than to the characteristics of their mostly rural origins.

Nineteenth-century immigrants came from the European countryside, though only a few remained farmers. Initially, the expansion of the frontier was in the hands of the native-born, accustomed to the difficult life that choice entailed:

> It was when the pioneer families departed that the immigrant farmers made their appearance. In the 1820's and 1830's they took over the evacuated lands in western New York, Pennsylvania and Ohio. In the 1840's they swarmed into Missouri, Illinois and southern Wisconsin. In the 1850's and 1860's they occupied eastern Iowa and Minnesota and consolidated their position in the older states. By the 1870s they had reached the prairies.[16]

The effects of the Homestead Act were such that: "The powerful appeal of free farms overshadowed caution and lured the immigrants at once to the frontier, for they wanted to get there before the land was all gone."[17]

Immigrants who remained tied to the land, however, were only a small part of an annual flow that exceeded 100,000 in 1842, 400,000 in 1854, 800,000 in 1882, and peaked at 1,285,349 in 1907 (a number equal to the combined populations of Nicaragua, Costa Rica, and Panama in that same year). A significant portion of these, for the most part peasants, went to work with pick and shovel as common laborers in mining or construction of the network of communication – canal, rail, and road – that grew ever vaster and more concentrated throughout the continent:

> Out of their labors came first the chain of canals, and then an intricately meshed network of railroads – by 1910, more than 350,000 miles of them. And these tasks were hardly completed before bicycle riders and motorists began to call for and to get a paved highway system: 200,000 miles were already laid by 1910.[18]

Nor was growth limited to railways and roads; the expansion of cities swollen by European migrants also created a significant labor demand.

> The increase of urban population strained the existing housing and created a persistent demand for new construction that kept the building trades prosperous. Everywhere streets pushed out into the suburbs where farms had once been: men's muscles had to grade the way, carry and fit the paving blocks. Each seaport dredged and improved its harbor, built imposing piers to accommodate the larger vessels of nineteenth-century commerce. Intricate systems of aqueducts, of gas pipes, of electric wires, of trolley tracks, supplied water and light and transportation for the new city millions.[19]

And this growth was largely fueled by the manual labor of immigrants coming from Ireland, Central and Eastern Europe, and Italy.

Toward the middle of the nineteenth century, innovations began to transform manufacturing and the entire productive system:

The older industries had disdained the immigrants; but the new ones, high in the risks of innovation and heavy initial investments, drew eagerly on this fund of workers ready to be exploited at attractively low wages. The manufacture of clothing, of machines, and of furniture flourished in the great commercial cities precisely where they could utilize freely the efforts of the newcomers, hire as many as they needed when necessary, lay off any surplus at will. A completely fluid labor supply set the ideal conditions for expansion.[20]

The engaging prose of Oscar Handlin's classic work, from which I have liberally extracted, describes the fundamental aspects of European immigrant labor – swept up in the larger process of globalization – better than a series of cold census statistics or quantitative analyses (which in any case confirm his claims). These general trends could be elaborated in many ways; perhaps it will suffice to point out that the tertiary sector was also growing, and so absorbing immigrants in the cities: independent traders, shopkeepers, artisans, and food service workers thrived, in part thanks to the services they offered to the new ethnic communities.

Two other aspects of European–American migration, both symptoms of the growing integration of the two continents, need to be cited. The first is a macro-phenomenon: the cycles of European demographic growth – owing to the delayed decline in fertility relative to mortality that is generally referred to as the "demographic transition" – translated with a quarter-century delay (about the average age of a migrant worker) into analogous waves of transoceanic migration. Emigration served to defuse the demographic pressure that a larger entry of young workers would have exercised on the European labor market. Moments of high natural increase in the twenties, sixties, and eighties led to emigration peaks 20–30 years later. The other transatlantic connection is a conjectural one: fluctuations in the US economy following the Civil War translated into similar fluctuations in European migration, thanks to a rapid and effective system of information, communication, and transportation.

O'Rourke and Williamson drew the following general conclusions regarding this "second globalization":

> The mass emigrations within Europe and between it and the New World overseas surely had a significant impact on labor markets at home, raising real wages, improving living standards, and eroding poverty. And just as surely, the mass migrations must also have had a significant impact on labor markets abroad. Compared with a counterfactual world without them, the arrival of new immigrants reduced real wages, raised poverty incidence, and lowered living standards for the previous immigrants and unskilled native-born workers with whom the new arrivals competed. Thus, mass migration was a force tending to create economic convergence among the participating countries, living standards in the poor emigrant countries being pushed up closer to living standards in rich immigrant countries.[21]

We might more cautiously suggest that, rather than leveling out living standards for the general populations, globalization instead prevented the European–American divide from becoming a gaping one. Indeed, we have already shown that the gap, when measured in terms of per capita GDP, did in fact widen in this period.

Through to the first decades of the twentieth century, economic integration influenced the global migratory system, and not just that of the North Atlantic discussed above, in complex ways. The various currents directed to Latin America – 7 million migrants to Argentina and Uruguay, 5 million to Brazil, 1 million to Cuba, and other minor streams to Chile, Peru, and Venezuela – in the period prior to the between-the-wars Depression were driven by causes and effects similar to the North Atlantic migration. In the case of Brazil, for example, European arrivals – first Italians and then Portuguese, Spaniards, and

Germans – were joined by Lebanese, Syrians, and Japanese, testimony to the truly global scale of the migratory system. Drawn by the availability of good land in the Southern states and by the demand for labor on the coffee plantations of São Paulo, these migrants also fed a growing urban and industrial infrastructure. In Argentina and Uruguay, immigration – mostly from Italy and Spain – played a fundamental role in the formation of the nation.

Globalization in this historical period offers a rich area for research. How did it affect other parts of the world? What were its mechanisms and consequences? In the British Empire, economic and political mechanisms created a diaspora from the Indian subcontinent toward other colonies: Burma, Ceylon, Malaysia, South Africa, the Caribbean. Indentured servants comprised a significant portion of this migration – estimated at 29 million for the century ending in 1940 – though the system itself was abolished in 1920. There were also many Indian traders and shopkeepers.[22]

The diaspora from southern China (Guangdong and Fujian) was similar: an estimated 19 million emigrants, largely under contract, spread throughout Southeast Asia, to British, French, and Dutch colonies, and to the Philippines (in addition to a smaller flow that went to America). Massive migration to Manchuria instead came from northern China, owing more to the "political" opening of vast tracts of land than to the mechanisms of globalization (see chapter 1, p. 11).

During the three-plus decades that separated the beginning of World War I and the end of World War II, integration processes underwent a profound reversal. Those processes are normally gradual ones that play out on multiple interacting levels – cultural, social, economic, and political – and migration both fueled and accompanied them. The wars instead introduced traumatic disruptions that could only be overcome with great difficulty, especially on the political level. Cultural, social, or economic links can be repaired fairly quickly, but political fractures heal more slowly. Between the wars, national economies barricaded themselves behind protective walls of tariffs, and, as we have already explored (chapter 6, p. 61), those walls also sought to block migration. Between the early 1920s and the early 1930s, all the American countries, North and South, significantly restricted immigration. Meanwhile, the Great Depression cut demand for foreign labor.

In the post-World War II years, the internationalization process revived. Between 1960 and 2010, the export of goods and services increased more quickly than GDP by a significant margin, evidence of the strengthening of international ties. This was true at the global level, for the entire American continent, and for the United States taken by itself. As a whole, world trade in 1970 amounted to 12.7 percent of production. By 2008, that figure had tripled, while the links between globalization and migration were multiple and pervasive. One of the principal characteristics of this historical phase, however (and as will be argued further below (chapter 9, pp. 111–12), has been the dual nature of policies pursued by states and international institutions regarding the exchange of factors of production. On the one hand, there has been a sustained move to lower tariff and trade barriers as they impact the flow of financial instruments, goods, and services, encouraged by the creation of a powerful, super-national regulatory organization (the WTO or World Trade Organization). On the other hand, strong migration restrictions have remained in place and indeed have tended to get stricter. It is this political disjuncture that explains the weakness of the forces for economic convergence in this recent phase of internationalization as compared to the earlier one. The effort to encourage integration and free trade between Canada, the United States, and Mexico by means of NAFTA (the North American Free Trade Agreement of 1994) has indeed combined the primary resources, capital, and knowledge of the two Northern countries with the abundant workforce of the Southern one, but it has done nothing to facilitate migration which has instead been blocked by restrictions only made harsher after September 11, 2001.

Returning to the question of migration itself, European economic recovery following the disaster of two world wars coincided with a temporary American reopening to new entries. Between 1945 and 1955, about 4 million European migrants went to Argentina, Venezuela, Canada, and the US; seen in broader perspective, it was the tail end of a century of transatlantic migration. After 1950, the American continent south of the Rio Grande together with the Caribbean became a region of emigration, reversing the positive net migration balance that had characterized that region ever since the first contact with Europeans. Net emigration from this vast region is estimated to have been only slightly negative in the 1950s (–0.5 million) and then to have grown steadily to –11 million in the first decade of the twenty-first century: an overall outflow over 60 years of 34 million people, as compared to population growth that was nine times greater. Up until the 1980s, the great immigration countries like Argentina and Brazil resisted the forces of internationalization by means of protectionist policies intended to defend their domestic markets. Military governments and dictatorships, moreover, produced heavy outflows of population, especially among the educated classes. Around 1950, the per capita income of Argentina, Uruguay, and Venezuela was greater than that of Italy, Spain, and other peripheral European economies. By 1970, instead, the situation had been reversed, and so the economic incentive to leave Europe had disappeared.[23]

In the US and Canada, this same period saw a steady inflow of population: for the decades 1950–2010, we can estimate net immigration at 51 million, about a quarter of population growth for the period, and so a significant contribution. Still more significant were the structural changes of these population flows – where they came from – as they brought about long-term changes in the social make-up of the population of North America, in terms of culture, language, religion, and the abilities and experiences acquired prior to migration. These changes are especially evident in the data on "foreign-born" population in the US, always a significant proportion of the total. Census figures allow us to trace out a periodization: between 1860 and 1920 – the period of greatest influx – the percentage of foreign-born ranged between 13 and 15 (and peaked in 1910). Their relative weight declined subsequently, as a result of the drop in immigration, and dipped below 5 percent in 1970; subsequently, that figure increased once again and reached 12.5 percent in 2009. One can make similar observations regarding the "foreign stock," those who are either born abroad or else maintain close family ties in other countries as one or both of the parents are foreign-born. This component of the population was about a third between 1890 and 1930. It dropped to 16 percent in 1970 and then grew again to 20 percent in 2000, and 25 percent in 2009. The change in the distribution of the foreign stock – almost entirely European till the middle of the twentieth century – is also notable. In 1960, three-quarters of the foreign-born were European, and another 10 percent were Canadian (and so of European origin); the rest were mostly Latin American and Caribbean. In 2009, 53 percent of the foreign-born were from Latin America and the Caribbean, 28 percent from Asia, and just 12 percent from Europe. The top eight nationalities of origin – over a million persons – were Mexico (11.5 million), the Philippines and India (1.7 million each), China (1.4 million), El Salvador (1.2 million), Vietnam (1.1 million), and Korea and Cuba (1.1 million each). The largest European group was that of the Germans, in sixteenth place. Expansion of the sources of immigration to Southeast Asia and Latin America has been the result of profound geo-economic changes and has altered the nature of migration flows.[24]

The internationalization process has also been linked to economic fluctuations and changes in the labor market:

the relative decline of agriculture and, to a lesser extent, manufacturing; the expansion of the tertiary and service sector; greater training demanded for many jobs; and, last but not least, the segmentation of the labor market, deriving from the native-born population's reluctance to take certain jobs. This evolution has influenced international migration in complex ways, resulting in specializations associated with certain sending regions. In the US, in 2009, about half of foreign-born workers were concentrated in manufacturing, construction, agriculture, and cleaning, as compared to only about a quarter of the native-born; foreign workers were instead relatively under-represented in management, administration, and education (a third as compared to a half of native-born). Yet the foreign-born workers were themselves far from a homogeneous group: almost half of all Mexicans were employed in cleaning, construction, maintenance, and production, as compared to just a seventh of those born in Southeast Asia, almost half of whom instead were managers, engineers, educators, and health workers, occupations that only employed one Mexican in ten.[25] The nature of migration, in terms of human capital, and the possibilities for adaptation and success depend on these differences in profound ways. As a result, migration favors both very basic activities (manual labor, domestic workers) and very specialized ones (a technician or computer worker), as those abilities are easily transferrable; while other intermediate activities (work in offices or the professions) require greater familiarity with the local environment, norms, and rules, not to mention language, and so are harder to transfer to a new national setting.

The richest countries tend to compete for the more highly skilled and innovative immigrants, a process seconded by selective immigration policies, shown, for example, by the heavy influx of immigrant university students into OECD countries: they numbered 0.8 million in 1975, 1.9 million in 2000, and 3 million in 2007 (of whom 0.6 million were in the US).[26] Although most of these students return to their countries of origin after completing their studies, they contribute to internationalization in two ways: they establish permanent channels of communication and exchange, and they also form a "reserve" from which the immigration countries can draw the most capable.

Four centuries since the first organized migrations to North America, the region's demographic and ethnic make-up has undergone numerous transformations. A population that was numerically insignificant in 1600 now approaches 350 million, and may reach half a billion in the second half of the century. The initially indigenous population gave way to British domination in the seventeenth century; British, German, and African in the eighteenth century; and pan-European in the nineteenth. At the dawn of the twenty-first century, it includes significant Asian, African, and Latin American components.

– 8 –

A Tumultuous Present and an Uncertain Future

2010–2050

This book opened with the bitter observation that, of late, the idea that migration serves as a motive force in society has generally been rejected. Instead, migration is seen as an uncontrollable agent of social change, the deformed tile of a mosaic that cannot find its place, a background noise that interferes with the normal hum of social life. That historic phase characterized by active policies to attract immigrants, to organize their flow, and to improve the conditions of arrival has ended. The White Australia Policy that offered favorable conditions to permanent immigrants from the United Kingdom and other European countries ended in the 1970s,[1] while the German policy aimed at welcoming *Aussiedler* – ethnic Germans descended from migrants settled in other countries, often centuries ago – was more the recognition of an historic debt than a true opening to immigration; the early 1990s, in fact, constituted a transitory moment as hundreds of thousands of people were "repatriated" from lands where their families had lived for generations.[2] And the policy welcoming Jews from the diaspora to Israel – from Europe, Asia, and Africa – was certainly a special case. Except for these examples, and perhaps a few other minor ones, states today regard immigration as a phenomenon to limit and regulate, to accept if absolutely necessary but certainly not to leave to the unfettered forces of the market, demography, and individual choice. In the pages that follow, we shall address three fundamental aspects of migration in the present century: the role migration has played in the globalization process and its derivatives in two distinct historical phases; the demographic and social situation in Europe, and whether it calls for the continuation of a steady inflow of population; and, finally, the political and philosophical bases – as opposed to the mechanisms – of immigration policies. The last point also entails consideration of the reproductive fitness of emigrants in European post-industrial society.

Regarding globalization and migration, we can usefully compare the first globalization of the nineteenth century with the second one that has occurred over the past 50 years. During the earlier period – 1870 to 1913 – exports from Western Europe grew from 8.8 to 14.1 percent of GDP and the migratory pattern followed rules suggested by classical economics: Europe, rich in labor but short of land, sent migrants to the Americas, which in turn were rich in land and short of labor.[3] This process produced positive effects on both sides of the Atlantic as respective standards of living became more similar:

> It might be useful to repeat what we have learned about the mass European emigration: almost all of the observed income convergence in the Atlantic economy, or what we are now calling the North, was due to this North–North mass migration, and that same movement also generated more equal incomes in the labor-abundant sending regions. It is important to remember this fact when dealing today with the second global century.[4]

It was a period during which the internationalization of the world economy followed the three classic axes: free movement of capital, goods, and labor. And, while the inequalities between the countries involved in the migratory process were narrowed, the same cannot be said – at least in the initial phases – for the inequalities between individuals in the immigration countries.[5] In North America, the Irish, Italians, and other immigrants from Southern and Eastern Europe occupied for a period of time the bottom rungs of the economic and social ladder, feeding – one would say today – new pockets of poverty and social exclusion. But that observation applies largely to the first generations of immigrants, and the inequalities rapidly vanished as time passed and the second generation became economically active.

Similar processes apparently also took place in other large countries that received European migration: in Brazil, for example, where the first Italian immigrants were attracted by the coffee boom but found themselves trapped in a subaltern existence. Over the long term, however, and so overlooking the great variability of individual cases, we can claim that migration has been an efficient tool in the fight against mass poverty. Living standards in the countries involved leveled out, and the "new poverty" that was created was a transitory and non-structural phenomenon. From an economic point of view, immigrants constituted an essential element in the economic development of the receiving countries. From a social and institutional point of view, immigration was generally encouraged and well received, as attested by the free availability of land (distributed at no cost in the US, Argentina, and Brazil) and the easy access to citizenship generally accorded to immigrants. There was of course discrimination, but in the context of societies already riven by profound social divisions. It should not be forgotten that the great European migration to the US and Brazil started when slavery was still practiced in both countries.

The second great globalization has been faster than the first – between 1950 and 2000, exports compared to GDP in Western Europe grew from 9 to 36 per cent – while it has also differed in significant ways: it has involved all five continents; the movement of goods, services, and capital has been more intense; and new "non-Western" actors have emerged. Meanwhile, the barriers to migration have limited the exchange of labor and put a brake on international mobility. Although some view the West as risking inundation by a mass of migration, that migration has in fact been modest. Between 1870 and 1913, Western Europe exported about 15 million people (subtracting returners), a figure about equal to the net immigration received in that same area (with double the population) in the period 1950–2000. In North America, net immigration in the decade before World War I was on the order of 1 million per year, more or less the number it attracts today with a population three times as large. The current globalization, then, more about goods and trade than about human resources, has had the effect of increasing, rather than decreasing, the differences between standards of living in the different parts of the world, expanding the gap between rich and poor. A few quantitative observations, albeit vague ones, support this conclusion. The West (the 15 countries of the EU before 2004, North America, Australia, and New Zealand) enjoyed a per capita GDP (expressed in terms of relative purchasing power) in 1950 equal to $6,300; that figure was $3,800 greater than in Latin America, $5,400 than in Africa, and $5,500 more than in Asia. By 2001, the Western per capita GDP had almost tripled to $22,800: $17,000 more than in Latin America, $19,000 more than in Asia, and $21,300 more than in Africa. The gap between living standards in the West and the rest of the world gradually widened during the half-century in question. And it is not only the absolute differences that have increased, but also the relative ones: per capita GDP in Latin America and Africa – in 1950 respectively 40 and 14 percent of that in the West – declined by 2001 to 25 and 7 percent. These are isolated elements, but they synthesize the increased inequality brought about by the recent history of globalization, inequality that in turn increases the pressure to migrate. We can identify, then, a poor world subject to multiple forces: the greater distance between rich and poor makes the advantages of migration ever more explicit; modest improvements in the poorest countries allow them to participate in the global migration system from which they had previously been excluded by their very backwardness; while improvements in the countries with incomes on the lower-middle range tend instead to lessen the pressure to emigrate as domestic living standards become more acceptable.

Pursuing this a bit further, studies have shown that when the salary ratio between receiving and sending countries drops below 5:1 or 4:1, migration pressure relaxes or disappears, even when the absolute wage difference increases.[6] There appears to be an exponential increase in the indirect costs of migration as the well-being of the sending country improves. Higher levels of education in particular amplify the perceived costs – social, psychological, and of affection – associated with separation from one's family, culture, and home. So, while an expanding economic gap between rich and poor fuels migration, social and educational advance pushes in the opposite direction.

One can then identify several levels of the propensity to migrate in terms of the associated costs and benefits. Residents of the poorest countries, those essentially excluded from the globalization process, have little opportunity or inclination to migrate, even though the benefits might be great. The cost of participating in migration is high, given a lack of the knowledge and resources needed to compete with those populations already migrating and so generally preferred in the receiving countries. This analysis can help us understand the situation in sub-Saharan Africa where, although poverty is extreme, migration to the rich countries has been limited. Once economic development gets under way, the relative costs of entering into the migration process (better education, increased ability to confront the expense of travel and settlement, etc.) decline compared to the benefits. Hence the situation in Asia where the poorest

countries (Afghanistan, Laos, Vietnam, Cambodia) have
been excluded from international migration, while countries experiencing strong development (Indonesia, Malaysia, South Korea, Thailand) have contributed to the flow
of migrants directed to the oil-producing states in Western
Asia.[7] In a subsequent phase, as higher levels of education,
moderate well-being, and expectations of further growth
are achieved, the relative cost of leaving home begins to
increase and the tendency to migrate decreases. That
mechanism largely explains the drop-off in migration from
Southern Europe to the richer Northern countries in the
1970s, the failed materialization of a westward exodus
following the collapse of the Soviet Union, and the weak
level of internal migration within the European Union in
spite of the persistence of significant income differentials.

How then is Europe to cope with the scarcity of human
resources it faces, a situation deriving from half a century
of demographic decline? The proposed solutions are politically driven and range between two extremes. On one side,
there is the model of a closed society that values above all
its deep traditions and seeks to maximize the productivity
of its declining human capital by promoting social policies
and ideals to prop up sagging fertility and limit the negative impact of an imbalanced age structure, an age structure that puts youth at a distinct disadvantage. In a society
of this sort, immigration is a marginal phenomenon and
bears little on the social fabric. On the other side, there is
the model of an open society, one that maximizes in the
short run the opportunities afforded by what is for now
an almost unlimited supply of immigrants, that invests in
integration policies and concentrates on governing a
change that is rich in both possibilities and tensions. These
two possible models are very different, and preference for
one or the other depends on complex motivations that can
be traced to history, culture, needs, and interests. They
correspond, moreover, to two different conceptions of
social continuity over time and a society's mode of reproduction. In the first model, a society's continued existence

is assured by the succession of generations and depends almost exclusively on biological reproduction (fertility). In the second, reproduction is both biological and social: the new additions to a society include both indigenous off-spring and also those who are recruited, admitted, or ultimately accepted into that society by means of immigration. In the developed world today, there are countries like Japan, where immigration is a marginal phenomenon (foreigners make up less than 1 percent of the population), and others like Australia, Canada, or Switzerland, where immigration plays an important role in social renewal (over 20 percent foreigners). There is no doubt that in the current historical moment, and in a context of economic crisis, the model of the closed society predominates, favored both by public and political opinion. Nonetheless, the fact that the closed model finds popular and political favor does not mean that it is generally realized, as a complex interplay of international relations, demographic decline, and economic circumstances work against it. European societies today, in fact, range between a "closed, but not too much" model and an "open, but only a little" one. In other words, Europeans would like a closed society but find themselves obliged to open it some. The end result may be the worst and most schizophrenic combination: a society that is in fact open but governed by policies intended for a closed one.

It may be useful once again to consult a few figures in order to better evaluate the European situation and its prospects. In 2010, the continent (Russia included) counted 733 million inhabitants. Without immigration, that number is estimated to drop to 700 million by 2030 and include both far fewer young people and many more old ones. The population between the ages of 20 and 40 would decline from 208 to 154 million (−26 percent). This age group accounts for both most immigrants and the majority of childbearing; it is also the peak age range for innovative work and the acquisition of new knowledge. Instead, the population over 65 would increase from 119 to 163 million

(+37 percent). This is necessarily a hypothetical situation as the assumption of "closed doors" is not a realistic one. The strong decline of the young population, and of the working-age population more generally, will create a "vacuum" that is sure to generate continued intense immigration. Nor is this process homogeneous: in some countries, fertility has remained moderate and the working-age population is more or less unchanged (France, Great Britain, Scandinavia), though those countries account for only about a fifth of the European population; while in others that account for about half (especially Spain, Italy, Germany, and Russia), the potential demographic decline is well above average. Consider the creation of wealth: it is possible that in some sectors a workforce reduced by a third may produce as much as or even more than the previous generation. Increased productivity has, in fact, functioned in just this way in most of the manufacturing sector. In other sectors, however, that will not work: for example, in the large sector devoted to the care of individuals, where productivity has increased little if at all. If we also consider cultural and knowledge production, social activities of various sorts, and family or interpersonal relations, the coming generations will not be able to refill the ranks of adults, and there is a risk that the size and perhaps also the cohesion of society will decline.

To what degree does European demographic decline signal a continued demand for immigration? For many European countries, unemployment is high and activity rates low, especially among women and the aged. This means that there is a labor "reserve" that could be drawn upon to augment production. Moreover, the abundance of low-cost immigrant labor allows for the continuation of some economic activities that otherwise would be restructured or resized. Investment then is neglected as salaries and productivity remain low and a significant segmentation of the workforce persists. This analysis suggests that continued substantial immigration is unnecessary as a drop in unemployment, political reforms that keep older people at work and increase the activity level of women, and improved productivity in some sectors should be enough to maintain growth without creating serious bottlenecks in the labor market.

European demography, however, does not support this scenario. Even if we predict a moderate recovery in fertility – which so far has not materialized – the long-run prospects are for significant decline. Assuming a "business as usual" hypothesis, the labor force will decline from 226 million in 2005 to 200 million in 2025, and 160 million in 2050. Preventing that decline would require radical changes: an increase of occupation rates to maximum levels (as currently experienced in a few Northern European countries), a leveling of the differences between men and women, and (above all) an increase of the retirement age of 10 years.[8] Under these circumstances, the labor force would increase from 226 million in 2005 to 248 million in 2025, and then decline to 236 million in 2050. Halfway through this century, three out of four persons aged 60 to 75 would still be at work – today the figure is one in seven – and the average age of workers would be about 50. Theoretically, this scenario is not impossible, and, while it is socially and politically unpalatable, the current crisis has convinced many countries to significantly raise the statutory retirement age. Yet, even if it should come to pass, an aging and stationary European workforce would have to compete with other economic systems surely more dynamic in terms of human resources. In the United States, for example, the workforce (assuming zero immigration, the current retirement age, and male–female balance of labor) would grow slightly (+3 percent) as compared to a dramatic decline in Europe (–29 percent), and with a much lower average age.

There are several more points worth making relative to the future of immigration in Europe. The first concerns productivity: presumably its increase will be slowed by the decline in younger workers and increase in older ones. It is true that we now live in a so-called "knowledge society" in which the physiological factors of age count less than they used to, but it is hard to imagine that productivity increases could compensate for the projected decline in human resources. The second concerns the increased demand for personal services, inevitable accompaniment to an aging population. As already noted, this sector demonstrates little potential for productivity increases; nor does it exert much attraction among the indigenous labor force. The third concerns the potential conflict between an increased level of labor activity for women, a reduction in social benefits, and fertility recovery. Even if we assume progressive policies that speak to the need to accommodate childbearing, child rearing, and work, the fact remains that increasing the activity rates of women will run up against an eventual limit. Finally, wealthy European societies seem to exercise a sustained demand for highly skilled activities in information technology, healthcare, and other technical professions. Meanwhile, other sectors that rely on unskilled labor – agriculture and construction – depend heavily on immigration for their survival, and it is unlikely that those sectors will once again attract native labor.

A large and wealthy society with a population of several hundred million, like that of Europe, might exercise attraction in a number of ways: it offers centers of culture and education for students and workers, encourages movement across its internal frontiers, increases the mobility of the employees of multinational corporations, and generates temporary migration for services and agriculture. Foreign communities instead establish "chain migrations" that tend to lower the costs of settlement and make finding work easier for new generations of immigrants. Finally, in the past 20 years, the working-age population of the European Union has increased at a good clip, coincident with increased immigration. Is it really conceivable that in the coming decades (and once the current crisis has passed) immigration will not increase as Europe experiences further demographic weakening?

We have addressed two of the three issues raised at the beginning of the chapter, emphasizing the inequalities between countries that derive from the globalization process and Europe's faltering demographic profile. Indeed, we find that the root causes of immigration not only persist but are strengthened. We have also seen (in chapter 6) that in the past several decades net immigration into Europe has increased considerably, and that brings us to the third issue. It is a difficult question and concerns immigration philosophy (more than immigration policy), the nature of the migrant, and what sort of fitness maximizes the advantages of mobility.

First, we should review how the foreign presence in Europe came to be and how it has grown. There have been basically three types of entry. The first is for work, with a contract or a permit to seek employment, and this has been the main conduit. The second regards family links: spouses, children, and other relatives are admitted for the sake of "family reunification," taking advantage of their relationship (more or less strictly defined according to different national legislations) with those who already reside legally in Europe. This category includes birth – except in those countries that are governed by *ius sanguinis* (according to which the child of a foreigner remains a foreigner) – and also family descent in those cases where citizens of other countries are allowed to return to the country of their parents or earlier ancestors (in some cases after multiple generations). The third route is that of unauthorized entry, one that in some countries has become heavily traveled. These are the three principal types to which we can add other minor ones that include people entering for study or for political asylum, and wealthy individuals who transfer their resources to a new country for the purpose of investment or simply to support their new life. Overall, European immigration has been divided up more or less equally between these three types, though with differences of course between various countries, differences owing to national policies but also to migration history, geographic location, and the changing nature of the labor market. For example, among authorized immigrants (the first two of the three categories), those coming for work account for one immigrant in six in France, but six out of ten in Portugal. And again among authorized immigrants, work and family reunification represent almost everywhere over three-quarters of those admitted. The rest (just 5 percent, for example, in Italy) include asylum seekers, students, and others. There are no reliable figures for unauthorized immigration, except in a few national cases, but official sources cite a figure for the entire EU (27 countries) of 5–10 million.[9]

Taking a broad view, the entire migratory system depends upon the labor market: unauthorized immigrants are almost always looking for work; authorized immigrants are admitted either to take up a job or look for one; and family members almost always join a worker. The labor market is the key. Immigration flows are a function of the demand for labor; and the ability to participate in the labor market or attach oneself to someone who does are the prerequisites for immigration. This comes as no surprise. The immigrant makes a calculation of costs and benefits, perhaps subconsciously or instinctively, regarding above all the possibility of improving his or her standard of living, the level of which depends first and foremost on the wages offered by that labor market. At the same time, the receiving country (at least theoretically) makes a cost–benefit analysis regarding what immigration brings to it. How will the immigrant's contribution in terms of taxes and fees compare to what he or she receives in terms of benefits? Which economic activities are hampered by a dearth of labor and so might benefit from increased immigration?

In those cases where the link between immigration and the labor market is tightest, economic cycles can play cruel tricks. Spain offers one such example: for years the construction sector drove the economy, supported by high demand and low interest rates. The recent crisis instead has created hundreds of thousands of unemployed, many of whom are immigrants. The government has attempted to remedy the situation by offering money to immigrants who agree to return to their home countries. The worsening of the crisis, however, has rendered these measures both very expensive and not very effective. In the past half-century, many countries – Germany and Switzerland 40 years ago, Italy today – have sought to balance immigration and economic cycles by gearing the issuance of work visas to the duration of work contracts. This approach, however, has serious limitations. In the first place, the system itself is not easily controlled: at one extreme, the temporary worker becomes permanent, as with the *Gastarbeiter* in Germany, and, at the other, the immigrant worker stays in the country after losing his or her job and so slides into the category of illegals. But, above all, the short-term immigrant has little interest in social integration and so almost by definition remains marginalized. There is also the problem, unresolved almost everywhere, of regulating migration flows. To do so requires projections of labor demand: how many positions will be open and what sort of qualifications will they require? The changeability and unpredictability of the labor market render these projections elusive. It may be possible to predict the need for workers in specific sectors that require special training. There may be a need, for example, for a certain number of nurses or doctors with particular specializations that the domestic educational system is not able to produce. Or there may be many parishes that lack ministers or a need for a certain number of crane operators, computer experts, violinists, acrobats, Chinese instructors ... But for most economic activities – which do not require highly skilled workers and which might absorb or discard workers according to the logic of the market and wages – it is difficult to gauge the amount of labor demand that has not been met by the indigenous labor force. This problem is especially acute in countries where (theoretically anyway) the potential labor deficit is very high (as, for example, in the case of Italy).

These considerations highlight the need for some radical changes, changes that are unlikely to come about spontaneously and so will almost certainly require political support. The first and underlying one is the need for policies that support childbearing and so encourage a degree of recovery in fertility; 20 years hence that recovery would translate into growth in the labor force. It would also allow us to look to the future with the assurance that, starting about 2030, there would be a gradual reversal of the current implosion. The second change regards social policies. It is well known that the weakness of public family welfare programs – the Mediterranean countries are at the bottom of the European list regarding transfer payments to families and children – is at the root of the high demand for immigrant labor in the areas of personal care. Much of this work, it is worth emphasizing, is carried out by unauthorized immigrants and so has a lower financial cost for families. The state chooses to close an eye to the phenomenon, two eyes to tell the truth. By passing up on the minimal revenue that might be derived from these workers (if they were legal), it "saves" on those measures that would lighten the burden on families: adequate day care, full-time school, services for the aged, and other financial transfers. This greedy (and unjust) approach to family welfare fuels the demand for foreign labor.

The third change – certainly the most difficult – concerns the gradual replacement of activities requiring a high input of labor with others requiring a high input of capital. And, while it would certainly be a strategic choice for Europe and for the countries that exert the greatest touristic pull, such as Italy and Spain, to become gigantic artistic-residential theme parks (already the case in much of Mediterranean Europe) for the rest of the wealthy world (or that part of it becoming wealthy, like China), in that case the service and construction sectors which employ large amounts of labor would experience explosive growth and so the demand for immigration would increase.

There is, finally, a fourth necessary change that concerns long-term immigration policies, policies that are also labor policies. As already mentioned, work is the key not only for those who arrive with an authorized contract or permit, and for most of their family members, but also for nearly all unauthorized immigrants, while the prediction of labor demand is difficult at best. These problems are dramatically amplified if we pass from a society in demographic equilibrium – where the demand is modest as compared to the native stock – to one experiencing demographic decline like much of Europe today. In most of Europe, immigration is not a short-term phenomenon responding to temporary bottlenecks or the needs of certain sectors. It is instead a structural one and contributes to populating and settlement. Segments of other societies are transplanted to ours and so are destined to become part of it. Gaps created in the native population are filled not only in terms of the labor force but also the complex social fabric. The million or so Romanians who, over a few years, have arrived higgledy-piggledy in Italy will in the long run become a part of Italian society: not just babysitters and construction workers (and a few fugitives from justice), but students, artisans, laborers, office workers, pensioners – men, women, and children. And, while the original motivation for immigration is work, around the worker a family takes shape: relatives who also seek employment, children who grow up, go to school, and sooner or later become Italian citizens. These immigrants may form compact communities or, certainly preferable, integrate themselves into the larger society (or perhaps find an intermediate solution). So we are contemplating not simply labor immigration, but immigration that leads to settlement, populating, and citizenship. Yet if this is the definitive result of every migration – whatever series of obstacles are encountered along the way – why do the receiving societies insist on viewing immigrants as temporary or, in any case, do not encourage their stabilization and the putting down of roots? It is time to recognize the need for a change in policy.

We need to adopt a different philosophy. We should not ask the immigrant "what do you know how to do?" or "what sort of work will you do in our country?" but instead "who are you?" and "what are your goals in life?". The admission of an immigrant should not depend solely on the existence of a job to be filled, but also on the quality of human capital, the ability and desire for inclusion. Immigration is not a temporary aid for an arthritic society that has difficulty moving itself, but instead a permanent transplant. A few countries – Australia, New Zealand, Canada – have long adopted policies of this sort. Others have done so more recently, such as Denmark and Great Britain, or plan to in the future. A series of factors contribute to assessment of a candidate's suitability for immigration: age, sex, marital status, education, special skills, and knowledge of the country's language, culture and political organization. The expected end result of this process of inclusion is citizenship, and indeed most immigrants attain that status.

There are of course great obstacles to achieving a philosophical change of this sort. The policies of many countries (including Italy) are deaf to such appeals and view immigration instead as nothing more than a temporary fix. Moreover, the conceptual and political difficulties inherent in such a change are great. There is a notable difference between those countries in the New World where immigration served to populate empty lands (or lands that had been made nearly empty following the crisis suffered by the indigenous population) and European countries that are chock full of people and manufactured goods, countries that might benefit from a balanced demographic winnowing. This is a serious consideration, but one that has been manipulated by those who view the situation in a superficial way and hold that the current demographic crisis will not bring negative consequences deriving from the enormous diseconomies it entails. And yet the experience of recent decades tells us that, even in Europe, immigrants, who were often first seen as temporary workers, have instead become an essential part of the social fabric.

A political change of this sort entails concrete difficulties. The first regards identifying which qualities of human capital, present in individuals or families, favor inclusion in the long term. However determined, this list must rigorously avoid elements of discrimination, even implicit ones. The second problem regards the evaluation or measurement of those individual qualities and characteristics. Some are easily verified, such as vital statistics (age, marital status, the presence of children), while others can be determined by means of appropriate tools (education, professional qualifications, economic resources). Others instead can only be measured indirectly (openness to coexistence and inclusion). It remains, moreover, to be determined if the identified qualities all need to be present at the moment of immigration or might instead be acquired subsequently. They might, for example, be measured or checked at certain intervals: when residency is confirmed, voting granted for local elections, and, finally, citizenship awarded. The third difficulty concerns determining the appropriate volume of immigration, a volume that should respond to an evaluation of long-term needs (making allowances for special situations that might arise). One might, for example, consider the advantages of avoiding a demographic decline that badly distorts the age structure of the population or excessively reduces the working-age population (keeping in mind that immigrants have higher activity rates than the native population), meanwhile judging the ability of the system to provide the resources and structures necessary to the processes of inclusion and integration. These difficulties are not insurmountable and are no greater than those associated with the current attempt to manage immigration flows, an attempt sanctified by law but in practice unenforceable.

Conservatives are unlikely to embrace these proposals. Even recognizing that immigration is a structural phenomenon and that in the long run immigrants become an integral part of society, they refuse to acknowledge its necessity. The idea of immigration as a temporary fix is easily peddled to an inattentive or poorly informed electorate, one easily convinced that perhaps tomorrow we shall no longer have any need for it. Yet criticism comes from the progressive front as well, since linking admission to an evaluation of the immigrant's individual qualities is necessarily selective. And selection can always be branded discriminatory, even when considerations of ethnicity, sexual orientation, religion, and political opinions are excluded from the process. These criticisms merit serious discussion, free of ideological constraints: the negative aspects of a selection process governed by clear and explicit rules should be compared to the inherent selection (explicit or implicit) exercised by other policies. For example, the quota systems currently in force in many countries and based on geographic origin exercise a sort of geopolitical selection that has little to do with the immigrants' successful integration into the receiving society. And, alongside an inclusionary-focused immigration program, there must needs be another for the admission of asylum seekers and others seeking humanitarian protection, a process that allows for neither selection nor evaluation.

This philosophical change – from immigration as prosthesis to immigration as transplant – must necessarily take into account the complexity of society. There will continue to be demand for seasonal or circular migration, and also individuals who choose to split their lives among several different countries. The immigration of foreign students who spend long periods attending university should be encouraged, as it offers an excellent response to the processes of internationalization. Different arrangements will need to be made for different professions, but these processes will in any case serve as an integral contribution to the primary function of immigration, namely, the strengthening of a weakened demographic and social fabric. That population fabric, failing in this historical period to reproduce itself biologically, has partially replaced biological reproduction with social reproduction, namely, immigration.

− 9 −

On the Move, in an
Orderly Fashion

On the slave ships that transported over 10 million Africans across the Atlantic − voyages that covered thousands
of miles and lasted weeks or months − 10 to 20 percent
of the imprisoned passengers lost their lives. In the second
half of the eighteenth century, ships leaving from Senegal
and Angola, headed to the Caribbean, lost "only" 2
percent of their human cargo.[1] The amount of 2 percent
is also the level of mortality suffered by those wretched
migrants who crossed the Canal of Sicily or the Straits
of Gibraltar between 2002 and 2008, trying to get to
Europe. The comparison offers a second paradox: while
for the slave trade we have documentation in the ports
of both departure and arrival that describes the numbers
who embarked and disembarked, we cannot say the same
for those now crossing the Mediterranean, so that 2
percent figure is a poor estimate of a tragic reality, one
whose precise dimensions are unknown.[2] And this tragedy
is taking place in the twenty-first century, in a sea traversed by countless boats and ships (merchant, military,
fishing, and pleasure craft), patrolled by radar and air-
craft, monitored by satellite, enveloped in an invisible
network of billions of radio and telephone waves; every

millimeter is charted: coasts, depths, rocks, islands, currents, and winds.

The preceding passage is meant to emphasize how far we still have to go to assign dignity and order to one of the fundamental human prerogatives: that of free geographic mobility, without harming the rights of others or fearing that one's own will be curtailed. The pages that follow will address three questions. The first concerns the scale of the current migration and seeks to establish that migration is a fundamental element of economic development, and not an accidental or pathological phenomenon that derives from the imperfect functioning of our society. The second concerns the evolution of policies and considers several measures of the "disorder" affecting migration today, and the costs that disorder inflicts on the migrants themselves and more generally on the collectivity. We have already made reference to one of the most dramatic of those costs. The third question concerns the need for international cooperation in the management of migration. We begin with the assumption that an orderly solution achieved by means of consensus would allow both the sending and receiving societies, as well as the migrants, to gain maximum benefit at minimum cost.

The international scale of migration is considerable, though our knowledge of it is sketchy. Ironically, we know more about the goods and merchandise that cross the frontiers of the 200 or so countries that make up the world – quantity, type, price – than we do about the scale and characteristics of the human beings who cross those same borders. The United Nations estimates international migration on the basis of census counts, namely, on the number of people classified in each country as "foreigners," or else born outside of the country in which they reside.[3] Using this imperfect measure (censuses always underestimate unauthorized migration), we find today (2010) a "stock" of migrants of about 214 million people (there were 191 million in 2005), or 3 percent of the population of the world. Half a century ago, that figure was just a little bit lower: 2.5 percent. Over the 20 years between 1990 and 2010 (subtracting the effect of border changes in the former Soviet Union and former Yugoslavia, which created artificial increases), the migratory stock in the world increased from 82 million to 128 million in the developed countries (from 7.2 to 10.3 percent of the total population), and from 73 to 86 million in the less developed countries (from 1.8 to 1.5 percent of the total population). About 10 percent of the population of the rich countries consists of immigrants: the experience of migration then is a common one. An unknown portion of this population has long integrated into the host society and so has presumably resolved many of the obstacles that make the immigrant life difficult. At the same time, there are other millions who still undergo the hardships of migration, including some who are born in the country chosen by their parents: namely, those second generations – and in some cases subsequent ones – who may be denied citizenship and so the rights that accrue to that status, or else continue to live in conditions of miserable segregation. It is impossible to measure the scale of these latter phenomena.

In addition to figures on the size of immigrant populations, there are other statistics – still less reliable – that seek to monitor in and out migration. The Organisation for Economic Co-operation and Development (OECD) collects official migration figures from its member countries. Counting only permanent immigrants (and so not seasonal or other temporary ones), these numbered 4.5 million in 2006 for the 27 OECD countries, countries that numbered about 1 billion inhabitants, including a migratory stock of about 95 million.[4] In that same year, these countries counted about 2.5 million permanent outmigrants, leaving a net gain of about 2 million. These are macro data that match other estimates and give an idea of the current scale of migration.[5] As we explored in chapter 8, in spite of the crisis these numbers continue to increase. For the sake of comparison, we might recall that the 1 billion inhabitants of the wealthy countries generate about 10 million births per year (their biological renewal), a figure that helps us to understand the current significance of immigration. For the year in question, there were 4.5 million immigrants and 10 million births, about one immigrant for every two births, though net migration (in-migration minus out-migration) was about 2 million or one migratory addition for every five births.

The preceding figures refer to only a single year, while the overall situation is changeable – so, during the recession years of 2008–9, they fluctuated. Nonetheless, these figures do help us get a handle on the larger picture. In the first decade of the twenty-first century, immigration has played an important role in the demographic renewal of wealthy societies as a whole, and that role is likely to increase in the decades to come, as we have tried to outline in the preceding chapter. Emigration is not a marginal or short-term phenomenon calling for temporary expedients, but is instead an essential and structural component of demographic, social, and economic renewal.

Yet, while the forces that generate migration remain strong, the barriers erected against it – both metaphorical and physical – are raised ever higher, in the hope of reducing international population flows. And yet a UN survey from 2007 suggests that only 19 percent of countries considered their immigration level too high that year, as compared to 41 percent in 1996.[6] A more careful look at current policies, however, reveals a contrary trend. In most of the wealthy countries, policies are becoming ever more restrictive with the introduction of measures too varied and complicated to describe here.[7] While immigration policies in the traditional immigration countries – the United States, Canada, Australia, and New Zealand – have not undergone dramatic changes over the past 50 years, those in Europe have instead altered in fundamental ways, starting with the zero immigration policies of the 1970s, and followed by the gradual relaxation of those policies, the growth of the European Union, the introduction of common policies for the policing of frontiers, and the reverberations deriving from the break-ups of the USSR and Yugoslavia. Nonetheless, we can identify some general trends: in the first place, the control or reduction of immigration levels by means of ceilings, quotas, or other similar policies; and, in the second, limitations to family reunification. Following on the zero immigration policies of the 1970s, it was primarily by means of family reunification that the migratory stock increased. The right of family members to join together is generally recognized, but the rules can be adjusted in various ways to modulate the inflow of population. Some countries, for example, have raised the minimum age at which a spouse can take advantage of family reunification, in order to prevent marriages of convenience. Others have increased the wage requirements for the resident sponsor requesting the reunification, or else increased the period of residence required before the sponsor (if a foreigner) can make a reunification request. Yet another trend has seen ever greater attention to immigrants with special qualifications: legal obstacles are relaxed, residency made easier, and exceptions to quotas allowed. Of special interest are medical workers, experts in applied technology, and other specializations. This latter trend is not restrictive in and of itself, but viewed more broadly it is, insofar as it is part of a thrust to limit the immigration of less qualified workers. As discussed in the previous chapter, selection criteria and a point system have been implemented in Australia, New Zealand, and Canada; similar systems are being tried in parts of Europe – the United Kingdom and Denmark – and studied elsewhere. Only those who accumulate a certain number of points – based on characteristics that might include age, family situation, knowledge of languages, professional qualifications – are considered as possible immigrants. The European Union is considering the introduction of a "Blue Card" that gives highly qualified foreigners easier access. Since 1965, the United States has had a quota for immigrants deemed to have especially desirable skills.

It goes without saying that these policies exercise a negative effect on the sending countries which lose in this way some of their most valuable human capital.

In the larger picture, attempts to limit the influx of foreigners have also translated into more restrictive policies on asylum seekers and those seeking to migrate for humanitarian reasons, with the result that those numbers have declined notably in recent years.[8]

A final observation concerns the growing preference in wealthy countries, by means of various policies, to encourage temporary or so-called circular migration: short-term migrations that, in one form or another, include return trips to the home country. The official justification for these policies is that they limit the "brain drain" on the sending countries and maximize the remittances sent home. There is also, however, an unofficial reason, but one no less important for that: namely, the conviction that labor demand, especially for unskilled work, can be satisfied by temporary migration. The presumed benefits then are of two sorts: on the one hand, the impact on public services, including healthcare and social assistance, is limited, while, on the other, the permanent immigration of unskilled and poorly educated individuals and families – held to be less likely to achieve social integration – is minimized. European institutions are supporting a so-called "coherent development policy" in which temporary and circular migration play a central role.

On the topic of circular and temporary migration, we can cite the important statement made by the OECD in its authoritative report on international migration in 2007:

> The expectation of temporary stay by labour immigrants does not appear to be a foundation on which one can construct a solid migration policy. Some labour needs, both high and lesser skilled, are of a permanent nature and need to be addressed by long-term migration ... Likewise, some returns of highly skilled migrants to their country of origin do occur and will undoubtedly continue to do so. But it is

illusory to expect that migrants will return just because they are able to do so without jeopardising their status in the host country. Little from recent migration experience suggests that this is a major phenomenon, especially when the entire family is involved and when economic conditions in the origin country remain difficult.[9]

The real problem is that policymakers have not found a way to prevent temporary migration – we'll use this abbreviation for that set of rules that link migration to a fixed-term contract, usually a fairly short-term one, after which it is expected that the worker returns to his or her country of origin – from becoming permanent. The history of the twentieth century is full of relevant examples. We might consider Mexican migration to the United States. In 1942, in the midst of World War II, the US and Mexico created the Bracero Program, so that seasonal Mexican labor could fill the gaps created in the US labor force by mobilization. A benefit to the US economy, the program continued for nearly two decades after the war, until 1964. About 100,000 Mexican workers traveled to the US each year, with peak levels of 400,000 reached in the late 1950s. Meanwhile, contrary to the intentions of the program, many of the temporary immigrants became permanent ones. And, although the program terminated in 1964, the demand for labor continued unabated:

> Some undocumented migrants eventually found a way, through marriage, education, or work experience, to qualify for legal status and to regularize their presence under prevailing migration law. Undocumented workers were found in jobs outside agriculture and far from the Southwest, including some even refurbishing the Statue of Liberty. Illegal migration became a national issue.[10]

So it would seem that once legal entry has been closed off, immigration simply continues by illegal means. The Hispanic community in the US today – largely Mexican and deriving primarily from immigration that has taken place since World War II – numbers 48 million, and so constitutes the country's largest "minority," more numerous even than African Americans. The Census Bureau projects that in 2050 the Hispanic population in the US will reach 103 million, and its share of the total population will jump from 15 to 25 percent. An impressive result for a group of seasonal workers brought in to pick grapes and tomatoes!

Germany offers an analogous example. Between 1945 and 1973, migrant workers were considered temporary: to recruit, employ, and then send back home as suited the employers:

> To enter and remain in the FRG, a migrant needed a residence permit and a labour permit. These were granted for restricted periods, and were often valid only for specific jobs and areas. Entry of dependants was discouraged. A worker would be deprived of his or her permit for a variety of reasons, leading to deportation. However, it was impossible to prevent family reunion and settlement. Often officially recruited migrants were able to get employers to request their wives or husbands as workers. Competition with other labour-importing countries for labour led to relaxation of restrictions on entry of dependants in the 1960s. Families became established and children were born.

This is how the Turkish community in Germany took shape, by far the largest foreign group in that country (equal to a quarter of the foreign population).

> Foreign labour was beginning to lose its mobility, and social costs, (for housing, education, and healthcare) could no longer be avoided. When the federal government stopped labour recruitment in November 1973, the motivation was not only the looming "oil crisis," but also the belated realization that permanent immigration was taking place.[11]

The pithy phrase of Max Frisch – "We asked for workers. We got people instead." – refers to the Swiss case, much like the German one, and well synthesizes the short-sighted view of many governments relative to immigration.

The tendency of immigration policies to become ever more restrictive in the wealthy countries reflects a change in public opinion. Whatever the merit of that opinion, there is today less tolerance of foreigners: greater concern about the potential threat immigrants may pose to national security, and less concern about discrimination; less recognition of the need for foreign labor, and greater fear of the competition and displacement it poses relative to national labor. Racism too rears its ugly head. Opinion polls, privileged observers, social surveys, and the press all reflect these changes, and policy – always more attentive to present concerns than long-term needs – follows suit. In Europe, significant increases in the average age of the population, weak economic growth in recent decades, and the shadow of the current crisis all contribute to public doubt regarding the positive role of immigration. The failure, or at best inefficiency, of present controls and the scale of unauthorized immigration only serve to confuse matters further.

A quarter of a century ago, the United States granted an amnesty (the International Regularization Control Act of 1986) that legalized 3 million foreigners; meanwhile, unauthorized immigration continued at a steady clip, estimated at about half a million per year. Official sources currently estimate the unauthorized stock to number about 12 million (equal to the entire population of Pennsylvania, the sixth largest state in the US). The problems posed by this population without rights grow greater every year and not only because their number grows larger; many of them have been in the US for long periods, have formed families, engage in normal economic activities, and are well integrated into American society. The life of undocumented immigrants is strewn with obstacles, made still more serious by local governments who in recent years have restricted access to public services, including schools, healthcare, permits of various sorts, and drivers' licenses. The Bush administration tried and failed to convince Congress to pass a bill that would at least partially resolve this immense problem.

In Europe, the most authoritative studies put the unauthorized population at 1–2 percent of the total; applying that estimate to the entire European Union yields an unauthorized population of between 5 and 10 million.[12] Europe presents a paradox: EU norms forbid mass expulsions just as they forbid mass amnesties. Each case, whether of legalization or expulsion, must be judged individually according to complex procedures that the various national judiciaries are unable to process when the numbers are high. An EU norm on repatriation contemplates incentives for immigrants who return home voluntarily. And yet, to take one example, legislation introduced in Italy as part of a "security package" (according to which unauthorized immigration is a crime) prevents the country from implementing this reasonable measure. The unauthorized immigrant who wants to repatriate voluntarily would in fact be immediately accused, condemned, and forcibly expelled. In the effort to combat unauthorized immigration, Italy deprives itself of a dignified escape route.

Finally, there is the case of the Russian Federation. Now that the flow of nationals who had in some sense been expatriated by the break-up of the USSR and the creation of new states has run its course, Russia is absorbing large numbers of unauthorized immigrants from central Asia and the Caucasus. A frontier that stretches for 20,000 kilometers is inevitably porous, if only for its length. Estimates of these new immigrants range from a minimum of 3–5 million to a maximum of 10–15.[13] Throughout the wealthy part of the world, one encounters no end of measures aiming to combat, reduce, or stop illegal immigration: strict border controls; walls, fences, and other physical barriers; military deployed on land and sea; monitoring from the air and electronic surveillance; not to mention the obsolete devices of passports and visas or the usually ineffective internal police controls.

Summing up the situation:

1   There are strong forces generating global migration flows: globalization, connections between cultures, the declining cost of travel, and, most of all, the growing economic and demographic divide between rich countries and poor. The recent economic crisis only makes the picture more complex.
2   Restrictive laws are enacted in wealthy countries in order to control the levels of legal immigration. In many countries, these laws favor specialized labor, altering the overall immigration profile, and also temporary or circular migration as an alternative to long-term settlement.
3   The number of unauthorized immigrants continues to grow, and attempts to stabilize or reduce it by blocking illegal immigration are often futile.

These trends combine to pit the interests of the receiving countries against those of the sending ones and in particular the main actors, namely, the migrants themselves. The sending countries bemoan the loss of their best human capital, though it is in their interest to encourage emigration among large and growing generations of young workers. At one and the same time, they complain about the obstacles blocking the integration of their nationals into host societies and the restrictions on family reunification, while recognizing that remittances are maximized when emigration is temporary and the migrant leaves family behind in the country of origin. Finally, the elite of the sending countries have long understood emigration to be a symptom of the failure of their own development policies. In the words of Ferruccio Pastore:

> In order to avoid confessing "political guilt," many governments of emigration countries have developed an

ambiguous discourse ... Those who leave in search of fortune are presented, depending on the moment and the circumstances, either as unfortunate and well-deserving children of the fatherland who are sacrificed for the collective good or else as potential traitors who have been exposed to the seductions of the West and so the temptation to forget their families and their traditions; the latter risks cutting them free of that network of obligations and loyalties that every migrant leaves behind.[14]

Immigration countries, on the other hand, complain that the sending countries fail to cooperate when it comes to limiting the departure of illegal migrants and are unwilling to accept those same migrants when they are deported. The true victims, of course, are the migrants themselves, lost in a labyrinth of laws and so unable to properly assess the advantages that may accrue to their decision to migrate, often in situations of illegality and so ones in which they are more exposed to exploitation. It is a commonplace to repeat that migration is a positive-sum game in which everyone stands to gain something. So it may be, but contrasting interests and policies, the lack of cooperation between countries – not to mention cases where government is simply absent – reduce the advantages that the various actors are likely to gain:

> Building beyond international cooperation toward international governance requires acknowledging that different states have different goals, compromising where possible, and building first on recognized common objectives – the need for more knowledge and understanding of migration phenomena, fewer deaths of migrants in transit, reduction of the influence of criminal networks, minimizing tensions between migrant and host communities, greater safety and dignity for migrants, increased national security, the maximum mutual benefit from migration, and a general capacity to implement policies that have been embraced.[15]

Yet what is the likelihood of achieving international governance? We have explored, as far as migration is concerned, the differences between the globalization of the late nineteenth century and that of the past half-century. In the latter period, social integration – of which an indirect index is the stock of migrants – has progressed less than economic integration, which can in turn be measured by the ratio of trade to domestic product. Economic globalization has been pursued by a long-term and coherent political and cultural program that includes the ever-freer exchange of goods, the lowering of trade barriers and tariffs, and the creation of a powerful international body able to regulate international commerce (the World Trade Organization). Meanwhile, the barriers to migration have been stiffened and the global forces that generate migration impeded. A shared vision of the common good has failed to materialize among international bodies, not to mention individual governments.

Few countries have ratified the conventions of the International Labour Organisation (ILO) that have to do with migrant workers (n. 97/1949 and n. 143/1975), while the measures provided by the United Nations, the International Convention on the Protection of the Rights of All Migrant Workers and Members of Their Families, adopted in 1990, took 13 years to be enacted and, as of mid-2009, had been ratified by only 43 countries (just one of those being in Europe). The interests in the conflict are too strong, the voice of the immigrant too faint, and the long-term understanding of common interests too weak.

In 2003, the UN Secretary General Kofi Annan created the Global Commission on Migration and Development (GCMD); after two years of consultation and debate, it produced in 2005 a proposal that was as timid as it was vague. That proposal consisted of the creation of an International Global Migration Facility (IGMF) that "could facilitate coordinated and integrated policy planning in areas that cross the mandates of several institutions, for example human trafficking, the migration asylum nexus and the developmental implications of international migration, including remittances."[16] In simpler terms, the IGMF is meant to coordinate the work of several agencies (though those agencies would each maintain their individual functions), some attached to the UN, such as the United Nations High Commission for Refugees (UNHCR), the ILO, and the UN agencies for refugees and for labor, and others outside of it, such as the International Organization for Migration (IOM), the WTO, and others. Yet even this modest project to coordinate functions scattered among different agencies is, after five years, a dead letter. As to the more ambitious goal "to bring together the disparate migration-related functions of existing UN and other agencies within a single organization and to respond to the new and complex realities of international migration," the final Report describes this as "a longer term approach."[17] In other words, one that is postponed to some vague and distant future date.

If even these minimal proposals have gotten nowhere, what can be said of the idea to gradually erect a supranational body – something like the WTO – to which fractions of national sovereignty (minimal ones at the beginning) can be surrendered in the area of immigration? Proposals of this sort gain little traction in international discussions and are associated with a few isolated voices:

> The world badly needs enlightened immigration policies and best practices to be spread and codified. A World Migration Organization would begin to do that by juxtaposing each nation's entry, exit, and residence policies toward migrants, whether legal or illegal, economic or political, skilled or unskilled. Such a project is well worth putting at the center of policymakers' concerns.[18]

Noted economist Jagdish Bhagwati wrote these words several years back. Few other voices have joined his chorus.

Leaving aside for now the juridically and diplomatically complex question of what an institution designed to regulate international migration would look like – whether a new and autonomous agency (a World Migration Organization) or an amalgamation of existing ones (for example, the UNHCR and the IOM); whether, within the ambit of the UN or outside of it and so on, we might instead start by asking what functions such an agency might perform? During an initial phase, we can imagine that it would carry out useful and non-controversial, or only mildly controversial, tasks: the gathering of data, analysis of existing and proposed policies, technical assistance and other services, the creation of an international forum for discussion and debate, and support for international negotiations and initiatives to combat human trafficking. These are relatively neutral functions, ones that do not raise major conflicts of interest and might serve as the basis for an institution intended to improve international cooperation. But other ones would have to be added if a degree of governance is to be achieved. Using a list developed by Kathleen Newland, these might include: "protection of migrants' rights, standard setting, immigration law enforcement and border control, compulsory returns, and facilitation of migration," areas for which "the divisions among states ... are [still] too pronounced for them to act as a basis for developing habits of cooperation at this stage."[19] We might also include questions relative to the identification of the migrant, certification of birth and nationality, age and marital status, education and professional qualifications, knowledge of languages, and criminal record. Additional functions might come to include: guarantees that remittances circulate freely with minimal costs and maximum security, that pensions earned are not lost, and that labor contracts meet some minimum standard; the promotion and support (and eventually enforcement) of bilateral and multilateral accords for family reunification and for the readmission to home countries of individuals who have been legally expelled; the creation of a sort of "dual nationality" that specifies the migrant's rights and obligations vis-à-vis both the home and emigration country; and above all protection of migrants' rights, both those who migrate legally and those tens of millions who are living illegally in foreign countries. As it is, in some cases even legal immigrants live in a state of semi-servitude, subject to blackmail as their passports are held by the authorities or their employers.

While the scenario outlined seems utopian, the need is urgent. Indeed, the EU is showing signs that it may soon recognize the need to go beyond purely nationalistic approaches to migration. At first the issue was how to defend EU borders from unauthorized immigration by creation of the Frontex Agency whose powers are being augmented, especially for patrolling the Mediterranean. Yet how can those borders be defended in the absence of a larger global approach – as of yet nearly unfunded – one that recognizes the need for an articulated partnership between sending and transit countries? The EU "Stockholm Program" outlines a five-year migration plan for 2010–14 and includes ambitious elements that range from granting legal immigrants rights comparable to those of EU citizens to the introduction of an immigration code that would elaborate common norms for family reunification, to better regulation of economic immigration, coordination of integration policies, and the adoption of common criteria for admitting those seeking political asylum or admission on humanitarian grounds.[20] Ambitious but not overly so; the program indeed does not go beyond "guidelines" and "common criteria" for "coordination," always respecting the autonomy of single countries relative to immigration decisions.

Over the past two decades (from 1988 to May 2011), Fortress Europe has certified 17,000 deaths of immigrants seeking to land there.[21] But that is only the tip of the iceberg, as many more migrants perish in obscurity while crossing deserts or embarking on treacherous sea voyages. Thousands more die attempting to cross the US–Mexico border, while little is known for other parts of the world. These are not victims of war, but of peaceful attempts to move from one place to another. Refugees in the world numbered 10 million in 2010, four fifths of them in developing countries. Pakistan holds more refugees than all the developed world combined. Nearly 1 million people per year request political asylum.[22] The scale of criminal trafficking – in workers, women, and children – grows in direct proportion with the pressure to migrate and the international anarchy in migration legislation. The quantity of conflicts, deviance, and extreme poverty linked to migration in the immigration countries is high. Unauthorized immigration, itself a product of inadequate migration policies, is a mass phenomenon that increases vulnerability and marginalization. To take Italy once more, hundreds of thousands of unauthorized immigrants there became criminals in an instant as a result of a legislative act. In the poorer parts of the world, mass expulsions of immigrants have been used as a powerful political tool.

Migration is a human prerogative, the effects of which are linked both to the qualities of the migrants themselves – their fitness, as we have discussed above – and the economic, social, and political circumstances in which it takes place. Global forces fuel migration, while conflicts of interest increase. And so the need for international cooperation and global governance becomes ever greater for that significant segment of humanity that finds itself on the move and crossing national borders.

Table 1 Population and per capita income (1990 PPP$) in world regions, 1500–2001

Region	1500	1600	1700	1820	1870	1913	1950	1973	2001
Population (millions)									
Western Europe	57	74	81	133	188	261	305	359	392
Eastern Europe	14	17	19	36	54	80	88	110	121
Ex-Soviet Union	17	21	27	55	89	156	180	250	290
North America, Oceania	3	2	2	11	46	111	176	251	340
Latin America and the Caribbean	18	9	12	22	40	81	166	308	531
Japan	15	19	27	31	34	52	84	109	127
Asia (without Japan)	268	360	375	679	731	926	1299	2140	3527
Africa	47	55	61	74	90	125	227	390	821
WORLD	438	556	603	1042	1272	1791	2524	3916	6149
Per-capita income (GDP in 1990 PPP$)									
Western Europe	771	890	998	1204	1960	3458	4579	11416	19256
Eastern Europe	496	548	606	683	937	1695	2111	4988	6027
Ex-Soviet Union	499	552	610	688	943	1488	2841	6059	4626

(*Continued*)

Table 1 (*Continued*)

Region	1500	1600	1700	1820	1870	1913	1950	1973	2001
North America, Oceania	400	400	476	1202	2419	5233	9268	16179	26943
Latin America and the Caribbean	416	438	527	692	681	1481	2506	4504	5811
Japan	500	520	570	669	737	1387	1921	11434	20683
Asia (without Japan)	572	575	571	577	550	658	634	1226	3256
Africa	414	422	421	420	500	637	894	1410	1489
WORLD	566	595	615	667	6875	1525	2111	4091	6049

Notes: The acronym PPP stands for "purchasing power parity." Since the mid-twentieth century, economists have employed methodologies that allow comparison of the volume of economic activity in different countries while eliminating the variations of local prices. Per capita incomes expressed in 1990 dollars are theoretically comparable in different countries and different years as the purchasing power of each dollar should be equivalent. Pre-twentieth-century estimates are largely inductive.

Western Europe: EU of 15, Switzerland, Norway.

Eastern Europe: The rest of Europe, excluding the countries of the former USSR.

Source: Angus Maddison, *The World Economy: Historical Statistics*. Paris: OECD, 2003, pp. 256 and 262.

Table 2 Net migration from Europe to the Americas, 1500–1760, by country of origin (1000s)

Country of origin	Before 1580	1580– 1640	1640– 1700	1700– 1760	Total
Spain	139	188	158	193	678
Portugal	93	110	50	270	523
France	0	4	45	51	100
Holland	0	2	13	5	20
Great Britain	0	126	248	372	746
Total	232	430	514	891	2067

Note: The data for Great Britain include German migrants transported on British ships.
Source: David Eltis, *The Rise of African Slavery in the Americas*. Cambridge: Cambridge University Press, 2000, p. 9 (table 1.1).

Table 3 Slaves transported to the Americas and Europe, by destination, 1450–1870 (1000s)

Destination	1451– 1600	1601– 1700	1701– 1810	1811– 870	TOTAL
North America	–	–	348	51	399
Hispanic America	75	293	579	606	1552
British Caribbean	–	264	1401	–	1665
French Caribbean	–	156	1348	96	1600
Dutch Caribbean	–	40	460	–	500
Danish Caribbean	–	4	24	–	28
Brazil	50	560	1891	1145	3647
Europe	150	25	–	–	175
TOTAL	275	1341	6052	1898	9566

Notes: The Spanish Caribbean is included in Hispanic America. After 1810, Hispanic America refers only to Cuba and Puerto Rico.
Europe includes the Atlantic Islands and São Tomé.
Source: Philip Curtin, *The Atlantic Slave Trade: A Census*. Madison: University of Wisconsin Press, 1969, p. 268 (table 77).

Table 4 Average number of transoceanic migrants, by place of origin, 1846–1940 (1000s)

Period	British Isles	Germany	Norway, Sweden, and Denmark	France, Switzerland, and the Low Countries	Italy	Austria, Hungary, and Czechoslovakia	Russia, Poland, Finland, and the Baltics	Spain and Portugal	Balkan countries	"Old migration" (cols. 1–4)	"New migration" (cols. 5–9)	European total
	1	2	3	4	5	6	7	8	9	10	11	12
1846–50	199	36	4	14	0	2	0	0	0	253	2	255
1851–55	232	75	7	18	1	4	0	6	0	332	11	343
1856–60	124	49	5	7	5	2	0	6	0	185	13	198
1861–65	144	44	10	6	8	2	0	6	0	204	16	220
1866–70	171	83	39	15	19	6	1	12	0	308	38	346
1871–75	194	79	22	15	23	11	5	22	0	310	61	371
1876–80	115	46	23	9	29	12	7	17	0	193	65	258
1881–85	228	172	58	23	64	35	17	65	0	481	181	662
1886–90	215	97	61	35	134	53	46	97	2	408	332	740
1891–95	128	81	48	17	150	68	72	109	2	274	401	675
1896–1900	81	25	22	10	166	77	56	102	5	138	406	544
1901–05	156	28	54	15	321	203	143	98	21	253	786	1,039
1906–10	235	26	44	18	402	265	212	185	50	323	1,114	1,437
1911–15	266	16	29	16	312	244	217	220	47	327	1,040	1,367

1916–20	101	2	11	9	127	12	8	121	15	123	283	406
1921–25	198	59	26	12	131	24	57	96	27	295	335	630
1926–30	162	54	24	13	89	23	76	75	40	253	303	556
1931–35	30	13	3	4	28	5	21	20	7	50	81	131
1936–40	33	17	4	6	24	6	21	27	9	60	87	147
TOTAL	15,060	5,010	2,470	1,310	10,165	5,270	4,795	6,420	1,125	23,850	27,775	51,625
%	29.2	9.7	4.8	2.5	19.7	10.2	9.3	12.4	2.2	46.2	53.8	100.0

Notes: The totals in the bottom row are the sums of each column multiplied by five. "Old" and "new" migration were terms used at the time in the US (where most of the European migration was directed) to distinguish between traditional British and Northern European migration and that which came from Southern and Eastern Europe and became the majority in the late nineteenth century.

Source: Dudley Kirk, *Europe's Population in the Interwar Years*. Princeton: League of Nations, 1946, p. 279.

Table 5 Net migration by decade in world regions, 1950–2010 (millions)

Period	More developed regions	Least developed countries	Less developed regions (excluding least developed countries)	Africa	Asia	Europe	Latin America and the Caribbean	North America	Oceania
1950–59	-0.1	-1.0	1.1	-1.3	1.6	-4.9	-0.5	4.2	0.9
1960–69	7.1	-1.5	-5.6	-2.2	0.0	1.0	-3.8	4.0	1.1
1970–79	12.2	-9.2	-3.0	-3.4	-4.1	3.9	-4.2	7.1	0.6
1980–89	13.1	-9.3	-3.8	-3.5	-2.9	4.0	-7.0	8.3	1.0
1990–99	25.7	-0.5	-25.2	-4.1	-13.2	9.9	-7.8	14.3	0.8
2000–09	34.0	-8.9	-25.1	-6.3	-16.0	18.4	-11.2	13.3	1.8

Source: World Population Prospects: The 2010 Revision. New York: United Nations, 2011.

Table 6 World stock of migrants, 1960–2005 (millions)

Year	World	Developed countries	Less developed countries
Millions of persons			
1960	75.5	32.3	43.1
1965	78.4	35.4	43.0
1970	81.3	38.4	43.0
1975	86.8	42.5	44.3
1980	99.3	47.5	51.8
1985	111.0	53.6	57.4
1990	154.9	82.4	72.6
1995	165.1	94.9	70.2
2000	176.7	105.0	71.8
2005	190.6	115.4	75.2
2010	213.9	127.7	86.2
Migrants (stock) per 1,000 inhabitants			
1960	25.0	34.0	20.8
1965	23.5	35.2	18.4
1970	22.0	36.5	16.3
1975	21.3	38.7	14.9
1980	22.4	41.7	15.7
1985	22.9	45.6	15.6
1990	29.3	71.7	17.6
1995	29.0	80.8	15.5
2000	29.0	88.0	14.7
2005	29.5	95.3	14.3
2010	31.0	103.0	15.0

Note: The "stock" of migrants is calculated using census data and refers to people counted in each country as born outside of the country or else as foreign nationals. See also chapter 7, n.24.
Source: United Nations, Population Division, 2011 (<http://esa. un.org/migration/>); accessed November 4, 2011.

Table 7 World and continental populations (1950–2050) according to UN estimates and projections (millions)

AREA	1950	1975	2000	2025	2050
	Population (millions)				
World	2,532	4,076	6,123	8,003	9,306
More developed countries	811	1,046	1,189	1,287	1,312
Less developed countries	1,721	3,030	4,934	6,716	7,994
Africa	230	420	811	1,417	2,192
North America	172	242	313	383	447
Latin American and the Caribbean	167	323	521	669	751
Asia	1,403	2,393	3,719	4,667	5,142
Europe	547	676	727	744	719
Oceania	13	21	31	44	55
	% distribution				
World	100	100	100	100	100
More developed countries	32.0	25.7	19.4	16.1	14.1
Less developed countries	68.0	74.3	80.6	83.9	85.9
Africa	9.1	10.3	13.2	17.7	23.6
North America	6.8	5.9	5.1	4.8	4.8
Latin American and the Caribbean	6.6	7.9	8.5	8.4	8.1

Asia	55.4	58.7	60.7	58.3	55.3
Europe	21.6	16.6	11.9	9.3	7.7
Oceania	0.5	0.5	0.5	0.5	0.6

Annual % increase

World	1.9	1.6	1.1	0.6
More developed countries	1.0	0.5	0.3	0.1
Less developed countries	2.3	2.0	1.2	0.7
Africa	2.4	2.6	2.2	1.7
North America	1.4	1.0	0.8	0.6
Latin American and the Caribbean	2.6	1.9	1.0	0.5
Asia	2.1	1.8	0.9	0.4
Europe	0.8	0.3	0.1	-0.1
Oceania	1.9	1.6	1.4	0.9

2025 and 2050: medium variant.
Source: World Population Prospects: The 2010 Revision. New York: United Nations, 2011.

Table 8   Foreign born in Canada, the US, and Argentina, 1870s, 1910s, 1960s and 2000s

	Canada	United States	Argentina
1870s			
Foreign Born (000)	594	5,567	210
% Foreign Born	16.1	14.4	12.1
% 1st country of origin	45.8	33.3	33.9
% 2nd country of origin	37.5	30.4	19.7
% 3rd country of origin	10.9	13.8	16.2
Name of first 3 countries	UK, Ireland, US	Ireland, Germany, Great Britain	Italy, Border, Spain
1910s			
Foreign Born (000)	1,587	13,516	2,391
% Foreign Born	22	14.7	29.9
% 1st country of origin	43.3	17.1	48.9
% 2nd country of origin	19.1	9.9	19.7
% 3rd country of origin	7.6	9	8.6
Name of first 3 countries	Great Britain, US, Ireland	Germany, Italy, Great Britain	Italy, Spain, Border
1960s			
Foreign Born (000)	2,844	9,678	2,604
% Foreign Born	15.6	5.4	13

% 1st country of origin	31.9	13	33.7
% 2nd country of origin	10	10.2	27.5
% 3rd country of origin	9.1	9.8	17.9
Name of first 3 countries	UK, US, Italy	Italy, Germany, Canada	Italy, Spain, Border
		2000s	
Foreign Born (000)	6,187	31,133	1,532
% Foreign Born	19.8	11.1	4.2
% 1st country of origin	14	27.6	60.3
% 2nd country of origin	11.6	4.9	14.1
% 3rd country of origin	7	4.3	8.8
Name of first 3 countries	China, India, Philippines	Mexico, China, Philippines	Border, Spain, Italy

Notes: % of 1st, 2nd, 3rd country refers to the percentage of foreign born originating in each specified country. Canada: dates are 1871, 1911, 1961, 2006. Russia in 1911 comprises Poland. Country % refers to "newcomers," arrived in 2001–2006.

United States: dates are 1870, 1910, 1960 and 2000.

Argentina: dates are 1869, 1914, 1960, 2001. "Border" refers to countries bordering Argentina.

Source: National Censuses.

Table 9 Region of birth of the foreign-born population of the US, 1790–2009

Year	Total population (000)	Total Black population (000)	Total foreign-born population (000)	Black population as % of total population	Foreign-born population as % of total population	% Distribution of Foreign Born by Region of Birth					
						Europe	Asia	Africa	Oceania	Latin America	North America
1790	3,929	757	NA	19.3	NA	NA	NA	NA	NA	NA	NA
1850	23,192	3,639	2,203	15.7	9.5	92.2	0.1	0	0	0.9	6.7
1860	31,443	4,442	4,135	14.1	13.2	92.1	0.9	0	0.1	0.9	6
1870	38,558	4,880	5,564	12.7	14.4	88.8	1.2	0	0.1	1	8.9
1880	50,156	6,581	6,676	13.1	13.3	86.2	1.6	0	0.1	1.3	10.7
1890	62,622	7,470	9,244	11.9	14.8	86.9	1.2	0	0.1	1.2	10.6
1900	75,995	8,833	10,331	11.6	13.6	86	1.2	0	0.1	1.3	11.4
1910	91,972	9,827	13,506	10.7	14.7	87.4	1.4	0	0.1	2.1	9
1920	105,711	10,463	13,911	9.9	13.2	85.7	1.7	0.1	0.1	4.2	8.2
1930	122,775	11,891	14,197	9.7	11.6	83	1.9	0.1	0.1	5.6	9.2
1940	131,669	12,865	11,595	9.8	8.8	NA	NA	NA	NA	NA	NA

1950	150,697	15,042	10,347	10.0	6.9	NA	NA	NA	NA	NA	NA
1960	179,326	18,871	9,678	10.5	5.4	75	5.1	9.4	0.4	9.4	9.8
1970	203,210	22,580	9,304	11.1	4.6	61.7	8.9	0.9	0.4	19.4	8.7
1980	226,545	26,495	13,193	11.7	5.8	39	19.3	1.5	0.6	33.1	6.5
1990	248,710	29,986	18,959	12.1	7.6	22.9	26.3	1.9	0.5	44.3	4.9
2000	268,554	36,419	31,133	13.6	11.6	15.8	26.4	2.8	0.5	51.7	2.7
2009	307,006	39,641	38,452	12.9	12.5	12.4	27	NA	NA	54.1	NA

Note: NA = not available.

Sources: Campbell J. Gibson and Emily Lennon, *Historical Census Statistics on the Foreign-born Population of the United States: 1850–1990.* Population Division, Working Paper no. 29, US Bureau of the Census, Washington, DC, 1999. 2000, 2009: US Census Bureau.

Notes and References

Chapter 1   Waves of Progress and Gradual Migration

1   Charles Darwin, *The Descent of Man*. New York: The Modern Library, n.d., p. 41.
2   Luigi Luca Cavalli-Sforza, Paolo Menozzi, and Alberto Piazza, *Storia e geografia dei geni umani*. Milan: Adelphi, 1997, pp. 124–5.
3   Ibid., p. 211.
4   Albert J. Ammerman and Luigi Luca Cavalli-Sforza, *La transizione neolitica e la genetica di popolazioni in Europa*. Turin: Bollati Boringhieri, 1986, pp. 82–3.
5   Albert J. Ammerman and Luigi Luca Cavalli-Sforza, "Measuring the Rate of Spread of Early Farming in Europe," *Man* 6/4 (1971): 674–88.
6   Cavalli-Sforza et al., *Storia e geografia*, p. 208.
7   Michel Rouche, "Le haut Moyen-Age," in Jean-Pierre Bardet and Jacques Dupâquier, eds, *Histoire des populations de l'Europe*, vol. 1, *Des origines aux prémices de la révolution démographique*. Paris: Fayard, 1997, pp. 143–4.
8   Massimo Livi-Bacci, *The Population of Europe*. Oxford: Blackwell, 2000. The material relating to this work in the preceding pages can be found in the second chapter, which can be consulted for additional information and bibliographical references.

9 Walter Kuhn, *Geschichte der deutschen Ostsiedlung in der Neuzeit*, 2 vols. Köln: Graz, 1955.

10 Hermann Aubin, "German Colonization Eastward," in *The Cambridge Economic History of Europe*. Cambridge: Cambridge University Press, 1966, vol. 1, p. 485.

11 Ibid., p. 455.

12 Michael R. Haines, "The White Population of the United States, 1790–1920," in Michael R. Haines and Richard H. Steckel, eds, *A Population History of North America*. Cambridge: Cambridge University Press, 2000, p. 324.

13 Ray Allen Billington, *Westward Expansion: A History of the American Frontier*. New York: Macmillan, 1967, p. 10.

14 Valerian V. Obolensky-Ossinsky, "Emigration from and Immigration into Russia," in Walter Wilcox, ed., *International Migrations*. New York: NBER, 1931, vol. 2, pp. 553–65.

15 Ping-Ti Ho, *Studies on the Population of China, 1368–1953*. Cambridge, MA: Harvard University Press, 1972, pp. 158–63. Immigration in the 1920s was estimated at 300–400,000 people per year.

Chapter 2 Selection and Reproduction: The Settler Effect

1 Massimo Livi-Bacci, *Conquest: The Destruction of the American Indios*. Cambridge: Polity, 2008.

2 A. Rosenblat, *La población indigena y el mestizaje en America*, Buenos Aires: Editorial Nova, 1954.

3 Massimo Livi-Bacci, "500 anos de demografia brasileira: uma resenha," in *Revista brasileira de estudos populaçao* 19/1 (2002): 141–59.

4 Hubert Charbonneau et al., *Naissance d'une population. Les français établis au Canada au XVIIe siècle*, Montréal: Presses Universitaires de l'Université de Montréal, 1987.

5 Adam Smith *The Wealth of Nations* (1776), London: J.M. Dent & Sons, 1964, vol.1, p. 63.

6 *Relazione sulla leva dei nati nel 1893*: out of 100 recruits examined in Italy, 20.9 were declared unfit and 26.6 temporarily unfit. The figures for the Italians examined in the US were 18.4 and 19.9. In addition to the natural selection attendant on emigration, there was also that imposed by

immigration authorities who subjected new arrivals to a medical exam before admitting them to the country.

7   Jacques Vallin and France Meslé, "The Segmented Trend Line of Highest Life Expectancies," *Population and Development Review*, 35/1 (March 2009): 171.

8   Massimo Livi-Bacci, *L'immigrazione e l'assimilazione degli italiani negli Stati Uniti*. Milan: Giuffré, 1961, p. 72.

9   This is what happened, for example, among the immigrant groups in Australia.

10 L. Toulemon, "La fécondité des immigrées: nouvelles données, nouvelle approche," *Population et Sociéte* 400 (April 2004). Gian Carlo Blangiardo, Maria Paola Caria, Alessio Menonna, Simona Maria Mirabelli, Livia Ortensi, Colombo Sciortino, and Laura Terzera, "Le aree di attenzione," in Gian Carlo Blangiardo, ed., *L'immigrazione straniera in Lombardia. Rapporto 2008*, Milan: Fondazione Ismu, 2009, pp. 152–60.

11 Livi-Bacci, *L'immigrazione*, pp. 64, 103.

Chapter 3   Organized Migrations

1   Catherine Julien, *Gli inca*. Bologna: Il Mulino, 1998, p. 82.

2   Clifford T. Smith, *An Historical Geography of Western Europe before 1800*. London and New York: Longman, 1978, p. 176.

3   Hermann Aubin, "German Colonisation Eastwards," in *Cambridge Economic History of Europe*. Cambridge: Cambridge University Press, 1966, vol. 1.

4   Joseph A. Schumpeter, *History of Economic Analysis. S.l.*, Taylor & Francis e-book, 2006 [1954], p. 241.

5   Isabel De Madariaga, *Russia in the Age of Catherine the Great*. New Haven and London: Yale University Press, 1981, pp. 361–2. For a complete history of the German people of the Volga, see Fred C. Koch, *The Volga Germans: In Russia and in the Americas, from 1763 to the Present*. University Park, PA: Pennsylvania State University Press, 1977.

6   Giuseppe Parenti, "Tentativi di colonizzazione della Maremma nel XVI–XVIII sec.," *Economia* XVI/1–2 (July–August 1937); Lorenzo Del Panta, "La vicenda delle colonie lorenesi in Maremma (XVIII secolo) come esempio di studio

di demografia differenziale," in A. Grassi, ed., *Statistica e demografia: un ricordo di Enzo Lombardo tra scienza e cultura*. Rome, Università di Roma La Sapienza, Facoltà di Economia, TIPAR, 2007, pp. 141–53.

7   Gonzalo Anes, "El Antiguo Régimen: los Borbones," in Miguel Artola, ed., *Historia de España Alfaguara*. Madrid: Alianza Editorial, 1983, vol. IV, pp. 142–3.

8   "Primeiras medida sobre e imigraçao e colonização," in Therezinha De Castro, *História Documental do Brasil*, Rio de Janeiro and São Paulo: Distribuidora Record, 1988.

9   Bartolomé de Las Casas, *Historia de las Indias*, 2 vols. México: Fondo de Cultura Económica, 2nd edn, 1995, vol. II, p. 226. (Partial English translation (not including this passage): Bartolomé de Las Casas, *History of the Indies*, trans. Andrée Collard. New York: Harper & Row, 1971.)

10   Sergio Della Pergola, *La trasformazione demografica della diaspora ebraica*. Turin: Loescher, 1983, p. 61.

Chapter 4   Three Centuries: 1500–1800

1   David Eltis, *The Rise of African Slavery in the Americas*. Cambridge: Cambridge University Press, 2000.

2   Paolo Malanima, *Energia e crescita nell'Europa preindustriale*. Rome: La Nuova Italia Scientifica, 1996.

3   Massimo Livi-Bacci, "Poplazione ed energia," in *Atti della XXXIV Settimana di Studi 2002. Istituto Internazionale di Storia Economica "F. Datini": "Economia e Energia secc. XIII–XVIII."* Florence: Le Monnier, 2003.

4   Carlo M. Cipolla, *Tecnica, società e cultura*. Bologna: Il Mulino, 1989.

5   Theodore C. Barker and Christopher I. Savage, *An Economic History of Transport in Britain*. London: Hutchinson University Library, 1974, p. 30.

6   Rondo Cameron, *A Concise Economic History of the World*. Oxford: Oxford University Press, 1997, pp. 172–5.

7   Jan de Vries and Ad van der Woude, *The First Modern Economy*. Cambridge: Cambridge University Press, 1997, p. 708.

8   Fernand Braudel, *Civilization and Capitalism, 15th–18th Century*. Berkeley, CA: University of California Press, 1992.

9   Massimo Livi-Bacci, *The Population of Europe*. Oxford: Blackwell, 2000, pp. 116–18.

10 Jan Lucassen, *Migrant Labour in Europe, 1700–1900*. London: Croom Helm, 1987. For Italy, see Carlo A. Corsini, "Les migrations internes et à moyenne distance en Italie: 1500–1900," in A. E. Roel and O. Rey Castelao, eds, *Les migrations internes et à moyenne distance en Europe, 1500–1900*. Santiago de Compostela: Commission internationale de démographie historique, 1994, vol. 1.

11 Hans Fenske, "International Migration: Germany in the Eighteenth Century," *Central European History* XIII/4 (1980): 332–47.

12 William H. McNeill, *Europe's Steppe Frontier, 1500–1800*. Chicago, IL: University of Chicago Press, 1964, p. 199.

13 Bernard Vincent, "Les migrations Morisques," in *First European Conference of the International Commission on Historical Demography*. Santiago de Compostela, 1993, vol. 1.

14 Jean-Pierre Poussou, "Migrations et mobilité de la population en Europe à l'époque moderne," in Jean-Pierre Bardet and Jacques Dupâquier, eds, *Histoire des populations de l'Europe*, vol. I, *Des origines aux prémices de la révolution démographique*. Paris: Fayard, 1997, pp. 262–86.

15 Ibid.

16 Huguette Chaunu and Pierre Chaunu, *Séville et l'Atlantique*. Paris: SEVPEN, 1956, tome VI, vol. 2.

17 Livi-Bacci, *Population of Europe*, pp. 120–1.

18 Livi-Bacci, "Popolazione ed energia," p. 117.

19 De Vries and van der Woude, *The First Modern*, p. 75.

Chapter 5 A Quickening Pace: 1800–1913

1   Paul Bairoch, "The Impact of Crop Yields, Agricultural Productivity, and Transport Costs on Urban Growth between 1800 and 1910," in Ad van der Woude, Akira Hayami, and Jan de Vries, eds, *Urbanization in History*. Oxford: Oxford University Press, 1990.

2   David B. Grigg, *The Transformation of Agriculture in the West*. Oxford, UK, and Cambridge, MA: Blackwell, 1992.

3   Blanca Sanchez Alonso, "Labor and Immigration," in V. Bulmer-Thomas, John H. Coatsworth, and Roberto Cortés

Conde, eds, *The Cambridge Economic History of Latin America*. Cambridge: Cambridge University Press, 2006, vol. II, p. 385.

4   Paola Corti, *Storia delle migrazioni internazionali*. Rome and Bari: Laterza, 2005, p. 34.

5   Francesco Colletti, *Dell'emigrazione italiana*. Milan: Hoepli, 1911, p. 233.

6   Maurice R. Davie, *World Immigration*. New York: Macmillan, 1936, pp. 452, 456.

7   Stanley C. Johnson, *A History of Emigration from the United Kingdom to North America, 1763–1912*. London: Routledge, 1913, pp. 39–40.

8   Emily Greene Balch, *Our Slavic Fellow Citizens*. New York: Charities Publication Committee, 1910, p. 49 (also republished in Oscar Handlin, ed., *Immigration as a Factor in American History*. Englewood Cliffs, NJ: Prentice Hall, 1959, p. 27).

9   Jean-Claude Chesnais, *La transition démographique*. Paris: Presses Universitaires de France, 1986, p. 181.

10 Philip Roth, *American Pastoral*. Boston, MA: Houghton Mifflin, 1997.

11 John Kenneth Galbraith, *The Nature of Mass Poverty*. Cambridge, MA, and London: Harvard University Press, 1979, pp. 120–1.

12 Douglas S. Massey, "The Social and Economic Origins of Immigration," *Annals AAPSS*, 510, July 1990, p. 66.

Chapter 6   The Last Century: The Trend Reverses, 1914–2010

1   Figures in this chapter on population growth and migration for Europe (and its subdivisions) after 1950 are taken from *World Population Prospects: The 2010 Revision*. New York: United Nations, p. 201.

2   On the topic of population losses during World Wars I and II, see Dudley Kirk, *Europe's Population in the Interwar Years*. Princeton: Princeton University Press, 1946, pp. 65–70; see also Jean-Jacques Becker, "Les deux Guerres mondiales et leurs conséquences," in Jean-Pierre Bardet and Jacques Dupâquier, eds, *Histoire des populations de l'Europe*, vol. III: *Les temps incertains 1914–1998*. Paris: Fayard, 1999, pp. 79–86.

3 Massimo Livi-Bacci, "On the Human Costs of Collectivisation in the Soviet Union," *Population and Development Review* XIX/4 (1993): 743–66.

4 Data on per capita income in Europe and its subdivisions in this chapter are taken from Angus Maddison, *The World Economy, Historical Statistics*. Paris: OECD, 2003. Maddison's estimates use "1990 international Geary-Khamis dollars," namely, 1990 dollars calculated in terms of purchasing power in order to allow comparisons between different eras and places.

5 Kirk, *Europe's Population*, p. 98.

6 Becker, "Les deux Guerres," p. 78.

7 Stephen Castles and Mark J. Miller, *The Age of Migration*. New York: The Guilford Press, 1998, p. 65.

8 Ibid., p. 63.

9 According to UN estimates (see n. 1 of this chapter), net migration for 1970–90 was +8 million.

10 In the Europe of 27, persons residing regularly in a country different from that of their citizenship (2005) account for about 5 percent (24 million) of the total; though a good third of these come from other EU countries. These latter then are European citizens and so entitled to free circulation; according to EU ordinances, they are not really "foreigners." The true registered "foreigners" number about 16 million, to which must be added an imprecisely known number of irregular non-EU citizens; official sources put their number at between 5 and 10 million for a total of 20 or 25 million.

11 The medium variant projections for 2010 included in *World Population Prospects: The 1998 Revision*. New York: United Nations, 1998, vol. 1, are: 55.782 million for Italy (p. 235) and 39.089 million for Spain (p. 371), for a total of 94.871 million. Official estimates by ISTAT and INE for 1 January 2010 are instead 60.5 million for Italy and 47.5 million for Spain.

12 Pursuing this idea, we might say that the impact of immigration can be estimated using an equation like the following:

$$\text{Impact} = [(I:P):D]:[(Y_e:Y_i) \times (P_e:P_i)],$$

where I is the stock of immigrants, P the receiving-country population, and D the length of the migratory process during which the stock I is constituted. So $(I : P) : D$ is the rate of immigration, Y_e and Y_i are per capita incomes in the countries of emigration and immigration, and P_e and P_i are the prerogatives (political, cultural, technological) of the migrants and of the receiving-country population.

Chapter 7   Three Globalizations, Migration, and the Rise of America

1   Population and income estimates and data are included in the tables in the Appendix and taken from the sources cited there.

2   Angela Brittingham, C. Patricia de la Cruz, *Ancestry: 2000.* Washington, DC: US Census Bureau, 2004.

3   Kevin O'Rourke and Jeffrey G. Williamson, *Globalization and History: The Evolution of a Nineteenth-Century Atlantic Economy.* Cambridge, MA: MIT, 1999, p. 2.

4   Charles H. Parker, *Global Interactions in the Global Modern Age, 1400–1800.* Cambridge: Cambridge University Press, 2010, p. 99.

5   O. H. K. Spate, *The Spanish Lake.* Minneapolis, MN: University of Minnesota Press, 1979, p. 289.

6   Luke Clossey, "Merchants, Migrants, Missionaries, and Globalization in the Early-Modern Pacific," *Journal of Global History* 1 (2006): 44.

7   Stuart B. Schwartz, *Sugar Plantations in the Formation of Brazilian Society: Bahia, 1550–1835.* Cambridge: Cambridge University Press, 1985, pp. 41–2.

8   James Horn, *Adapting to a New World: English Society in the Seventeenth Century Chesapeake.* Chapel Hill, NC, and London: University of North Carolina Press, 1994.

9   David W. Galenson, "The Rise and Fall of Indentured Servitude in the Americas: An Economic Analysis," *Journal of Economic History,* 44/1 (March 1984): 1–26.

10   Angus Maddison, *Monitoring the World Economy, 1820–1992.* Paris: OECD, 1995, p. 61.

11   Ibid., p. 64.

12   O'Rourke and Williamson, *Globalization,* pp. 124–32.

13   Angus Maddison, *Contours of the World Economy, 1–2030 AD,* Oxford and New York: Oxford University Press, 2007, p. 383.

14 M. R. Davie, *World Immigration*. New York: Macmillan, 1936, p. 44.
15 Ibid., pp. 309, 322.
16 Marcus Lee Hansen, "The Immigrant in American History," in Oscar Handlin, ed., *Immigration as a Factor in American History*. Englewood Cliffs, NJ: Prentice Hall, 1959, pp. 45–6.
17 Ibid., p. 46.
18 Oscar Handlin, *The Uprooted*. Boston, MA: Little, Brown and Company, 1979, p. 61.
19 Ibid., p. 62.
20 Ibid., p. 66.
21 O'Rourke and Williamson, *Globalization*, p. 145.
22 Adam McKeown, "Global Migration, 1846–1940," *Journal of World History* 15/2 (June 2004): 157–8.
23 Andrés Solimano, *Globalization, History and International Migration: A View from Latin America*. International Labour Office, Working Paper no. 37, Geneva, 2004, p. 3.
24 For definitions and statistics on "foreign born" and "foreign stock," see Campbell Gibson and Emily Lennon, *Historical Census Statistics on the Foreign Born Population of the United States: 1850–1990*. Washington, DC: US Census Bureau, Population Division, 1999; US Census Bureau, *Profile of the Foreign Born in the United States: 2000*, Current Population Reports, December 2001. For a 2009 update, see the following site: <http://www.census.gov/population/www/socdemo/foreign/cps2009.html> (extracted 24 February 2011).
25 For the distribution by occupation of the "foreign born", see the following site: <http://www.census.gov/population/www/socdemo/foreign/cps2009.html> (extracted 24 February 2011).
26 OECD, *Education at a Glance 2009*. Paris: OECD, 2010.

Chapter 8   A Tumultuous Present and an Uncertain Future: 2010–2050

1 Stephen Castles and Mark J. Miller, *The Age of Migration*. New York: The Guilford Press, 1998, pp. 75–6.
2 Ibid. p. 192.

3 Once again, except where noted, the macro-economic and macro-demographic data in this chapter are taken, respectively, from the works of Maddison and the UN (see chapter 6, nn. 1 and 4).

4 Jeffrey G. Williamson, "Winners and Losers over Two Centuries of Globalization," Cambridge, MA: NBER Working Paper no. 9161, 2002, p. 31.

5 Ibid.

6 *World Population Monitoring 1997: International Migration and Development.* New York: United Nations, 1998, p. 152.

7 Ibid., pp. 150–1.

8 Massimo Livi-Bacci and Johannes Koettl, "The Demography of Europe, ECA and MENA Countries, 2000–2050," Report to the World Bank, 2005.

9 On the themes touched upon in this chapter, see also *International Migration Outlook: SOPEMI 2009 Report*. Paris: OECD, 2009, and editions of the same publication from previous years.

Chapter 9   On the Move, in an Orderly Fashion

1 Philip D. Curtin, *The Atlantic Slave Trade: A Census.* Madison, WI: University of Wisconsin Press, 1969, p. 279. These data refer to slave ships coming from Nantes: eight gathered slaves in Senegal during the period 1748–52, and nine in Angola, 1788–92. Throughout the eighteenth century, however, losses were generally much higher, fluctuating between 5 and 20 percent (ibid., pp. 139–41).

2 Massimo Livi-Bacci, "Relazioni pericolose," *Neodemos*, 2009, at: <http://www.neodemos.it>.

3 United Nations, *International Migration Report 2006*, at: <http://www.un.org/esa/population/publications/2006_MigrationRep/report.htm>.

4 These data are taken from *International Migration Outlook: Sopemi 2008*. Paris: OECD, 2008, pp. 295–6. The 27 countries referred to received 4.5 million official immigrants (not including transitory and temporary migration); those countries include 19 from the EU (not including the three Baltic states, Slovenia, Cyprus, Malta, Romania, and Bulgaria) plus Norway, Switzerland, Turkey, Australia, New Zealand,

Canada, the United States, and Japan. In 2010 these countries counted 1.042 billion inhabitants.

5   The figure of 2.5 million departures (2006) is calculated using statistics taken from OECD, *International Migration Outlook*, p. 296, for 16 of the 27 countries listed in the previous note that collected that data. In those countries the ratio of departures to arrivals equals 0.55 (4.5 * 0.55 = 2.475 million net migration). An estimated immigration balance of about 2 million finds support in other sources. We have also noted that the stock of migrants over the period 1990–2005 grew by 33 million (or 2.2 million per year) for the developed countries (including Russia and other countries formerly part of the Soviet Bloc), a figure again compatible with the one calculated here.

6   *World Population Policies, 2007.* New York: United Nations, 2008, p. 64.

7   For documentation on these policies, see the OECD Reports cited above, in particular OECD, *International Migration Outlook: Sopemi 2008*, pp. 224–89.

8   Eight OECD countries granted asylum to between 500,000 and 600,000 applicants per annum over the four-year period 1999–2002. That number was halved in 2006 (282,000). Ibid., p. 315.

9   Ibid., p. 20.

10   Frank D. Bean, Georges Vernez, and Charles B. Keely, *Opening and Closing the Doors.* Washington, DC: The Urban Institute, 1989, p. 10.

11   Stephen Castles and Mark J. Miller, *The Age of Migration.* New York: The Guilford Press, 2009, p. 100.

12   *International Migration Outlook: Sopemi 2009.* Paris: OECD, pp. 121–2. In a recent European Commission document, unauthorized immigrants were estimated at 8 million, 1.6 percent of the population of the EU (Commission of the European Communities, *Justice, Freedom and Security since 2005: An Evaluation of the Hague Program and Action Plan* – COM(2009) 263 final, p. 6).

13   Irina Ivakhnyuk, *Migrations in the CIS Region: Common Problems and Mutual Benefits.* United Nations Population Division, International Symposium "International Migration and Development," 28–30 June 2006, Turin, Italy.

14 Ferruccio Pastore, *Dobbiamo temere le migrazioni?* Rome and Bari: Laterza, 2004, p. 41.
15 Kathleen Newland, "The Governance of International Migration: Mechanisms, Processes, and Institutions," Global Commission on International Migration, September 2005, p. 17.
16 Global Commission on International Migration, *Migration in an Interconnected World: New Directions for Action – Report of the Global Commission on International Migration.* Geneva, 2005, p. 77.
17 Ibid., p. 75.
18 Jagdish Bhagwati, "Borders Beyond Control," *Foreign Affairs* 82/1 (2003): 104.
19 Newland, "Governance of International Migration," p. 7.
20 See the preparatory document (dated 23 November 2009) for the Council of Europe on December 10, 2009, no. 16484/09, JAI 866.
21 See: <http://fortresseurope.blogspot.com/>. Over 2,000 victims have been counted by the same organization in the first six months of 2011, mainly a consequence of migrants fleeing from Libya.
22 *2010 Global Trends.* Geneva: UNHCR, 2011.

Index

Page numbers in *italics* refer to tables.

CPSIA information can be obtained
at www.ICGtesting.com
Printed in the USA
FSHW020159150119
55027FS